Palaces

and PRISONS

Books by

DOROTHEA STRAUS

Thresholds

Showcases

Palaces and Prisons

Palaces

and PRISONS

DOROTHEA STRAUS

HOUGHTON MIFFLIN COMPANY BOSTON
1976

Copyright © 1976 by Dorothea Straus.
All rights reserved. No part of this work may be
reproduced or transmitted in any form by any means,
electronic or mechanical, including photocopying and
recording, or by any information storage or retrieval system,
without permission in writing from the publisher.

Library of Congress Cataloging in Publication Data
Straus, Dorothea.   Palaces and prisons.
1. Straus, Dorothea—Biography.   2. Authors,
American—20th century—Biography.   I. Title.
PS3569.T6918Z52   1976   813'.5'4   [B]   76-26102
ISBN 0-395-24671-7   STR
Printed in the United States of America

v   10   9   8   7   6   5   4   3   2   1

TO ROGER, MY SON

*The difficulty lies in the fact that only
two realms are accessible to us, thinghood
and personhood . . .*

Abraham Joshua Heschel,
Who Is Man?

*They say that "home is where the heart is."
I think it is where the* house *is and the
adjacent buildings.*

Emily Dickinson, letter
to Mrs. Elizabeth Holland

CONTENTS

Palaces

and PRISONS

The Dream

The QE 2 was scheduled to sail at noon. Midmorning in New York City and the sky was an ominous yellow gray, December, the air as steaming and polluted as August, the buildings alight with night electricity. Inside the hermetically sealed glass compartments of their automobiles the drivers peered out uncomprehendingly, like preserved fish in individual deep freezers. What was awry with time?

The ramshackle docks in the Hudson River were vacant, only the Cunard Line sign was a familiar flare in the confused and murky scene. The smokestacks of the QE 2 rose above its shed, but something had gone wrong with them also, the tall bright columnar funnels had been turned into squat black irregular shapes resembling giant robot toads.

The passengers were starting to arrive. The QE 2 was chartered for a cruise to North Africa with the Young Millionaires' Club, a group of American businessmen who had made a minimum of a million dollars before reaching the age of forty. One looked in vain for the steep boarding gangplank that used to bridge the space between pier and ship, but there was only an airless interior perforated by one small opening, the inconspicuous entrance to the vast terrain of the QE 2. The travelers trudged toward this dark hole. It swallowed couple after cou-

ple. One abnormally tall man limped alone, his leg imprisoned in an iron brace. Despite their youth, the marchers were listless, the men looked undifferentiated and weary. But the equipment hung about their persons was shining and triumphant: the best in cameras, carryalls and portable radios which continued to murmur a litany of fresh political news and disasters.

Inside the successive lounges, stretching as far as the eye could see, the air conditioners were already working full blast, although the chandeliers were hung with Christmas tinsel; poinsettias, like palm trees in flame, were sprouting among the elephantine plush settees of the salons. The young millionaires and their wives headed for their assigned accommodations, the men unseeing, somnolent, as though their energy had been transfused into their flashing accouterment, the wives possessed by an irritable undirected vitality. As they stepped across the threshold of the QE 2 they were met by the insolent penetrating stare of two dark eyes.

Leopold Litvak was posted at the entrance to greet the passengers. As they filed past him he handed them a card, his name thickly embossed in rococo script with his title: "Culture Professional." Successful novelist and lecturer, he had been engaged at great price to hold classes on Russian literature. Between New York and Casablanca the young tycoons would become acquainted with Tolstoi, Dostoevski and Pushkin. Like blind men, the millionaires fingered the card to make sure of its expensive engraving, but no one seemed to notice its funereal black border. The attention of the women was riveted on Litvak himself. He was dressed in a bold brown and yellow plaid suit, fitted tightly to his slender fleshless body and although his back was ramrod straight, he looked poised for flight. His raven's head, crowned by a crest of black curls above a low, broad brow, was proudly held. He had a beak nose and a cruel, thin-lipped mouth. His blazing eyes seemed to have an independent existence of their own, their brilliance raying beyond his face as though some power had jerked them free from their deep wide-set sockets. The women shivered in response to those glowing coals that expressed neither warmth nor anything human but had a supernatural intelligence. Leopold Litvak bowed low and touched his thin lips to the bejeweled hands of the millionaires' wives. It was as though he were devouring all their glitter.

When everyone was inside, Litvak descended to his own cabin. Here the air conditioning stopped, and galvanized heat replaced mortuary cold. But impervious to temperature, he did not even remove his closely fitted plaid jacket. As elegant in privacy as he had been in public, he sat at his desk piled high with books and papers: stock market reports, tomes on cartels, insurance companies and advertising agencies. Tolstoy, Dostoevski and Pushkin were nowhere to be seen. Litvak opened a ledger and made an entry in his journal: "The voyagers appear to be ignorant of their fate. They embark, confident that they will return to the security of their homes. They do not know that deserted rooms harbor shadows forecasting decline and eventual oblivion. I am on board to instruct in my own fashion." At this point he was interrupted by the foghorn emitting its traditional parting blast. To the travelers it sounded off-key, the warning croak of a hidden nightmare monster. It would be best to flee, but there were no exits — only that sudden transmigration, the expulsion from dreaming to waking.

HOME BASE

WHENEVER I PASS my brother's house nowadays, I avert my eyes. But I always manage to catch a glimpse of its white-washed brick, ivy-smothered exterior and the steep steps leading down from the terrace to the expensive, neglected tennis court and swimming pool below. Although conventional and suburban, its like repeated many times throughout the Westchester area, the house is set apart for me. The trees and overgrown bushes bordering the driveway seem to be conspiring to hide in their bottle green, mottled shade all but fragmented sections of the rosy brick and white trim. The sign bearing my brother's name has only recently been taken down. The trucks parked inside the entrance, the new family preparing to move in are imposters. They are repairing the dilapidated roof, the leaks and the peeling paint, products of years of unpaid bills. The house is abandoned, at last, by my brother, whose bones are disintegrating in a neighboring cemetery, its small-town simplicity an inappropriate repository for his remains. This spacious, luxurious home to which he clung through all his adult life would be a more suitable tomb. There it stands, and I resent its implacable indestructibility, reminding me of the endurance of material objects and the frailty of human life. My brother, his stubborn will overcome, is dead at fifty-six and I am the sole survivor of a family that had once seemed to me to be the entire world.

Only now, after many years, I realize that my brother's house in Rye resembles our childhood home in nearby White Plains, sold when he was eight and I six, at the time my family took up their summer travels in Europe. My very first memory of my brother is placed against this background rather than New York City, where we spent more time. It finds me in my wicker go-cart, accompanied by my nurse, waiting on the road for the return of my parents from Lenox, Massachusetts, where they had been vacationing with my brother. The setting, the gestures, the inexplicable emotions are a dumb show in memory, the words and the interpretation having been added at later dates. In the rear is the brick Georgian house. On the road, cars are rare: the year is 1919 and I am two years old. At last the tall automobile we have been waiting for appears, stopping at the sight of us. I see the familiar faces of my mother and father with my brother between them. I seem to be lifted by excitement out of the go-cart. I am hugged and kissed as though one week's holiday had been a long and hazardous separation. The high car is home, and in a reversal of things, I feel that I am the returned traveler. Through the warmth of welcome, suddenly, I am aware of my brother's presence. I shrink from him, my parents' laps grow less alluring. It seems to me now, looking back, that even at that age I had been fighting the yoke that attached me to my brother. But then and later, obscure shame rather than jealousy had been the motivating emotion.

Retrospection is inaccurate, jumbling sequences, borrowing knowledge from later years. But when I study the snapshots from those prehistoric days, my beliefs are confirmed.

In one of them Philip is standing by my pram, his long fair Little Lord Fauntleroy curls framing a pretty face. But even then his eyes were wild and frightened and I can detect on the bridge of his nose the large tan birthmark that he bore all his life. In later years it appeared to me like a sign, a kind of stigmata that stood for all the pain his nature caused him to undergo. He is clutching the handlebars of my carriage. And still an infant, I already appear to be disavowing Philip. Chubby and bonneted, I am sitting up very straight, with my face turned away from him.

A later picture has also been preserved. It shows a group of children posed in a Swiss valley against snowcapped Alps. My brother and I are both wearing sweaters with Indian designs and we are holding identical Alpine sticks. But is it an accident that we are placed at opposite sides of the photograph, separated by the band of forgotten playmates? Or rather, is this the result of my ceaseless maneuvering? He is now unnaturally tall and lanky, no longer the pretty Little Lord Fauntleroy of the earlier snapshot. But his eyes are unchanged: still wild, still frightened, with the look of a runaway horse about to bolt, destroying anything or anyone blocking his passage.

Another photograph has come to me since his death. It moves me now. This time we are shown seated side by side in the cockpit of a fake airplane, a studio *trompe l'oeil* in Paris. My brother is wearing a man's dated fedora and I a flapper's straw cloche. We both stare into the lens. In the pilot seat his back is to me, but our ridiculous hats seem to unite us. They stand in some way for shared experience, a common age and environment.

On looking back, my childhood seems to have been largely composed of blocking my ears against the screams and retching in the next room — my brother's method of getting his way — and the occasional sobbing brought on by the brutality he inspired in his peers at school. I closed my eyes to his awkward gangling person, with his long spindly knicker-clad legs. Also I was careful to avoid his affectionate overtures to me: to respond might put me in danger of growing to resemble him. I realize now that those unwittingly self-serving cold tactics developed in me at an early age a superstructure, a protection against vulnerability. Perhaps it has been useful. But it was engendered by fear, fear of the loss of self-control, fear of apartness, fear of fear itself and, most of all, shame because of the consanguinity I was constantly attempting to repudiate.

I felt no jealousy at my father's Old Testament pride in his son. It was Philip who won the most elaborate presents, concessions and privileges. But I knew that they had been obtained by those wild screams and gagging sounds and so I was pleased by more moderate portions. My father, a small compact man, regarded his towering offspring with admiration tinged with disbelief. But all his efforts to lead Philip in his own path ended in failure.

At our country house my father enjoyed early-morning horseback riding. Before leaving for his office in the city he would mount his gleaming chestnut hunter, Wotan. I loved the sight of my father, spurred and booted, vaulting adroitly into the saddle. His homely swarthy face was newly shaved and immaculate; I knew its fresh smell and its smoothness against my cheek. Soon he purchased a smaller horse for Philip so that he might be accompanied on those morning rides by his son, his pride and joy, granted late in life after he was forty. But disaster always seemed to follow my brother. That June day started with deceptive innocence: a shiny early summer sun over fragrant new-mown lawns and the daisy field beyond the house. It was suddenly sundered by the violence of the accident. I don't believe that I was a direct witness to any part of it, but the facts reaching me indirectly in hushed snatches of dialogue I was not supposed to overhear were as shocking as the actual sight. I could picture Philip, unconscious, transported to the hospital where his blood-saturated jodhpurs were ripped off and the gaping wound in his stomach stitched closed, as crudely mended as one of my broken dolls. Later I learned that his horse had kicked him as he was clumsily trying to climb into the stirrups. This episode put an end to my father's morning rides with Philip but it did not discourage new projects. Both Philip and my father were optimists.

Early in life my brother learned that he could defend himself by the use of money — bribes and barter — and he retained this philosophy to the end of his days. Money — inherited, amassed, squandered, displayed — was power. Everything might be had for a price: toys, prestigious accommodations in hotels, ships, trains — even human beings and sexual love. His inflammable innocent's imagination presented beautiful women to him as flawless high-priced jewels. The actress Wendy Barrie was the first, and his attempt to purchase her established a pattern that was to be repeated again and again.

Although I was seventeen years old at the start of the Wendy Barrie incident, it was kept from me as scrupulously as the shocking riding accident long before. But again piecing together the fragments that reached me I was able to make a whole. That summer we set off for Europe as usual. We were accompanied by my cousin, Ben, the son of my mother's sister. She and her husband had lost their money in the stock market crash and although the sisters had never been congenial, duty was strong in their family and Ben often joined us on our summer travels to benefit from the advantages his wailing mother proclaimed they could no longer afford. But Ben possessed other advantages: he was handsome, sturdy, and had long golden eyes and the regular features inherited from the maternal side of his family. And most advantageously, he was an athlete. Next to my jerky loose-limbed brother he appeared a veritable Greek discus thrower. He had a cold clear intelligence and he often seemed to be sneering at both his own family and ours. He and my brother were an oddly assorted pair. Although midway between our ages, Ben largely excluded me from his notice. During an earlier summer at the seashore, my gender had made me the central figure in our games of post office. But this sport was soon outgrown and Ben's only use for me consisted of occasional grudging but expert whirls on a polished dance floor of some ocean liner or grand hotel. Although I had little affection for him, it was a relief to have a partner other than my stumbling gawky brother who always stepped heavily on my toes, crumpled my dress in his maladroit clasp and drowned the music by his incessant chatter.

I often wondered what Philip and Ben had in common — Ben, silent and secretive, Philip open and garrulous; Philip hysterical, Ben coldly controlled; Ben adored by girls, Philip uncertain, often rejected. That summer in their shared cabin and hotel rooms I noticed stacks of movie magazines. But these seemed no more significant than the pornographic novel *Bubu of Montparnasse,* secured in Paris the year before. At each stop on our travels Ben and Philip had attempted to leave the book behind so that it should not be discovered by my parents. And at each hotel the chambermaid had found it and repacked it in a valise. Once in their effort to disembarrass themselves of *Bubu,* they hid it under the mattress. It had still been retrieved. Ben must have been the instigator, because Philip remained oddly prudish about sex. The women who ignited him were enthroned in his fancy like vestal virgins in a temple of sham purity. His house in Rye came to be a holy cage for three of these unfortunates: his wives.

On our return from Europe, on fall weekends home from college, there were scenes behind closed doors. The noise of screams and retching had been replaced by violent shouting. Philip was being opposed. But as usual, my father capitulated and my mother would emerge pale and defeated. Now I realize that my brother was always an insurmountable barrier between my parents. In miniature, like the tiny landscape viewed inside a toy Easter egg, I again saw the old-fashioned automobile arriving from Lenox, Massachusetts, and the welcome sight of my parents returning. Between them sat my brother, a wedge, unremovable though not yet comprehended. The shouting abated. Philip departed for Hollywood, Don Quixote armored in money. But it was some time before I made the connection between this romance and the stacked movie magazines in the European hotel rooms. Philip had discovered the dainty feline features of Wendy Barrie in one of those cheap glossy photographs and had fallen in love with the image. He had determined to buy it with money extorted from my father and he set out to woo a woman he had never seen in the flesh. A fortune was dissipated in the process, which lasted several years, but the transaction was never completed: Philip was unable to purchase his obsession.

During this period I became engaged and married and my mother died. I have always felt that her end was hastened by those earthshaking battles and her futile attempts to oppose, alone, my brother and father. I see her as she

was at that time, shaken and distraught, already undermined — although I did not know it — by the illness from
which she died. To me Philip seemed to be the only illness, one shared by the whole family. On the eve of my
marriage my mother came to me. In spite of the opacity of
my self-absorption it was painful to see her still beautiful
face ravaged by an anxiety that eclipsed its radiance as completely as it smothered her natural intelligence and hu-
mor — like a dense gray fog blotting out the light of day.

"Philip is going to marry the movie actress Wendy Barrie," she told me, "but it does not concern you. You do not
have to have anything to do with him. I will not have him
ruin your life also."

Now I realize what a strange statement this was. She
loved Philip, perhaps all the more because of his trials. But
her insecurity caused her to be disloyal to her son and unsure of me, as though it were possible for me to lose my
own identity in my brother's bizarre love life. I recalled the
pretty catlike face of Wendy Barrie as it had looked out from
the pages of the movie magazines. It seemed remote and
unreal, powerless to injure me. But Philip was always most
real and present and my mother's words reinforced my habitual disgust and alarm harbored since infancy. My
mother did not live to see the collapse of the Wendy Barrie
affair and she was spared what was to follow.

It was about 1941, coinciding with the United States entrance into World War II, that Philip, always uncoordinated,
became a virtual cripple. Heavy iron and leather braces appeared on his long legs, causing him to clank like a robot as
he walked. Necessary or not—they were meant to correct
short tendons—they vanished after a decent interval following the end of the war. Now he had grown very stout. His
shirt collar was too tight, giving his face with its large aqui-

line nose still bearing the birthmark, the full lower lip and the vulnerable green gold-flecked eyes, the look of an apoplectic, sated Roman emperor. His bulk was overwhelming, but extreme thinness or fat were two sides of the same coin: the corporeal expression of his excessive nature.

He had joined his father and uncle in the family business, the Rheingold Brewery, founded in Brooklyn a century before. Sentimental and ceremonious, Philip worshiped tradition as long as it did not interfere with his personal desires. He would talk endlessly about Ludwigsburg, the little German town where his great-grandfather owned the local brewery, as though it had been an ancestral shrine. In some measure, that continuing river of golden beer helped to give him the security that his unsuccessful relationships had undermined at an early age. Jewishness was another handicap that fretted him more than the iron braces on his legs. Perhaps this was the reason for his early support of General Franco—what other Jew at that time had espoused the Spanish fascist side? Later, he would join the Catholic Church, motivated in part, I believe, by a similar desire to be included where he might have been excluded.

In business dealings, I heard of his brilliance from all sides. In one way this pleased me by mitigating my habitual shame, but I was shocked also. Was it possible that this tornadolike force might possess a brain? I did remember from our childhood the ease with which he could memorize an entire railroad schedule, including the foreign names of each town en route. But it was years before I understood that his mind, an extraordinary mechanism, was totally divorced from his feelings; that he could focus with precision on useless matters while his judgment remained uninfluenced—that he could be at once a brilliant operator and an emotional imbecile. At this time he created a business coup that was to give him a reputation lasting throughout his life. He had been put in charge of advertising at the brewery and one day the invention of the Miss Rheingold beauty contest sprang from the clutter of his mind like a synthetic Venus rising from the surging sea of American business. His exaggerations, volubility, credulity and extravagance made advertising his natural milieu and soon Miss Rheingold invaded the land, her white-toothed smile proliferating on billboards, newspapers and magazines. She became a celebrity in her own right: a multifaced Galatea and my brother, Pygmalion, her creator.

One winter in Palm Beach my husband and I witnessed the inauguration of the first, and most dazzling, Miss Rheingold, Jinx Falkenberg. Styles in beauty alter as much as fashions in clothes and now the image of Jinx Falkenberg might look as dated as the "spectator sport" costumes she used to pose in. But then she was perfection: a tall outdoor type with glowing skin and breeze-tossed chestnut curls. She was photographed holding water skis, snow skis, tennis rackets, baskets of flowers, kittens, puppies—on yachts, next to expensive convertibles, poised on diving boards and swings — and always her brown eyes sparkled and her cherry lips parted, smiling at the prospect of a glass of golden, frothy, refreshing Rheingold beer! That session in Palm Beach must have resembled an old Hollywood set: Jinx, the star, attended by her retinue: her photographer, Paul Hesse, small, dapper, black-mustached; her ambitious mother-wardrobe mistress-duenna; and overall, her impresario, my brother, enthroned in a director's chair. I recall my father, in the role of backer, somewhat eclipsed and bewildered, but proud of his son. And Philip was in his element, his disappointments and frustrations forgotten, surrounded by expensive equipment, basking in the warm

Florida sun, the golden ambiance of resort luxury and big business.

Following Jinx Falkenberg, a new Miss Rheingold was crowned each year. Occasionally Philip would select one upon whom to lavish one of his courtly crushes but it was not from their ranks that he picked his first wife. Norma Terry was a model also, but a more refined species, formed by the snobbish and sophisticated world of fashion photography. At the time of their marriage her face was familiar on the pages of *Vogue* and *Harper's Bazaar*.

Summoned to the tower suite of the Waldorf Astoria, my husband and I were accompanied by my father, disgruntled that this was his first knowledge of the elopement and, perhaps, uneasy at what he might find. It was to be expected that Philip had selected the most expensive rooms and a wife to match them. Norma was wearing a sleek black silk dress, with a design in torquoise that seemed to glow like phosphorous. She was thin, small-boned, scrupulously tidy and there was something bloodless about her perfectly modeled white face and small chiseled features. Her eyes were a glossy jetlike black and her shapely mouth, as carefully outlined as a tapestry rose, expressed extreme self-control. Later I realized how nervous she had been at this meeting but she showed no sign of it nor was there any indication of joy over the event we had gathered to celebrate. Pleasure registered on that immobile face would have been as unlikely as a chip in the perfect emerald she was wearing on the third finger of her left hand. She spoke little and when she did her voice was low-keyed and ladylike. Philip bridged the silences, recounting noisily their elopement to Maryland, the reluctance of "little Miss Norma" — and, with triumph, her capitulation at last. He always valued a conquest in proportion to his difficulties in obtaining it. He bragged endlessly about Norma's seven-year-old son, Douglas Smith. It was only then that I detected a softening in her eyes.

"He has been at boarding school because of Norma's work," my brother explained, "but that is all over now. We are starting tomorrow to hunt for a country house and Douglas will come home at once."

So the house in Rye entered our lives. I remember each part as I first viewed it complete: a long formal sunken drawing room with French doors opening on one side on the terrace and at the end a garden surrounding a fountain in the form of an Italianate cherub. The chairs and sofas were upholstered in chintz patterned with cabbage roses; tall gilt-framed mirrors reflected the stiff furniture display resembling the tower suite of the Waldorf Astoria. The staircase to the bedroom floor was graceful, wide, curving, banistered in white-painted wood and mahogany with a high window and a seat beneath it on the landing, midway, duplicating the White Plains home of our childhood. Did my brother also store in the attic of his memory the luxury of that bench beneath a great window and the sight of a curving staircase rising and descending from that perch like the view from a hospitable halfway chalet upon the side of a Swiss alp? The den was conventionally snug with leather furniture, and Philip had hung in the place of honor over the mantle a stern portrait of his maternal grandfather, whom it was said he resembled. The rumpus room was made to look like a tavern and contained Philip's collection of beer mugs. But he was especially proud of the oval Adam dining room painted pearl gray like the inside of an oyster. The table was appointed in English china, silver and etched crystal like the "best service" of our childhood home. Norma Terry presided dourly at that table, frowning, but not enough to damage her smooth forehead, while Philip exuberantly tried to instruct his beautiful new acquisition on how to comport herself in a fashion to match his memory of his mother.

Of course, Douglas was there: a ready-made son to complete the suburban family group. He was handsome, with Norma's delicate features, and the sullen expression in her black eyes was repeated in his gray ones. But like a *Saturday Evening Post* cover boy, he was suitably sloppy in frayed blue jeans and worn sneakers. To complete the picture Philip had given him a calico cat and a Sealyham terrier, upon whom my brother bestowed the exotic name of "Carmencita," in honor of General Franco's only daughter.

For Douglas, Philip built the swimming pool beneath the terrace. It is drained now, almost concealed by overgrown planting, and an ugly modern house has been constructed adjacent to it. Then it was alive with the duckings and splashings of Douglas and his friends. Philip, who in his childhood had always watched sports as an outsider with admiration untinged by envy, never nearer to a team than in the role of water boy, now boasted about Douglas's skills on the baseball field or basketball court. Norma never used the pool.

Of what was she thinking, idle within the house, captive for eleven years? Did she miss the harsh lights of her career? Was she remembering her early days as an elevator operator in a Chicago department store or her brief, impoverished, never-mentioned marriage during the Depression? When I look at the stylized photographs in fashion magazines I am reminded of Norma, although the androgynous, rangy, casual aspect of today's models resembles in no way her prim, flowerlike feminine appearance. But she was like a rose without its scent. For Norma scorned men. I pictured her heart, like her shapely mouth, perfect but inanimate. Just as those tight Japanese paper blooms unfold in water, it did open to children. And she had concern for women, all sisters in their victimization by men. I try, in vain, to re-create her against the interior of the house in Rye but, like the undented cabbage-rose chintz cushions in the rarely used drawing room, her existence seemed to have left no mark there. I see her dimly on the terrace, dressed in pristine white. Her thin body is rigid and her voice is bitter as she says, "At least your brother isn't like other men, he is humble" — or addressing me with sad superior wisdom: "I hope you never wake up, my dear — "

Douglas was the exception. For him she endured the boredom, disgust and unhappiness. I used to wonder how she would survive his emergence into that hated being: a man. In the meantime she accepted, ungraciously, all the material advantages my brother showered on Douglas: the private schools, the expensive athletic equipment, the wealthy friends. In order to insure his future Norma permitted Philip to legally adopt Douglas, but she did not permit her husband to give his name to her son. Yet my brother's generosity increased in proportion to Norma's growing scorn and discontent.

It was during Douglas's first term at Yale that Norma's eleven-year endurance gave way and she suffered a severe nervous breakdown, followed by a divorce from my brother. For a while, always prejudiced against Philip, I continued to see her high up in her immaculate expensive cold lonely Manhattan apartment, paid for by undeserved alimony, where she waited, loverlike, for her weekly telephone call from Douglas. She had been firm against my brother's insistent hysterical entreaties for reconciliation. Her tolerance for him had been exhausted and besides, as

Philip's legal son, Douglas would have everything he could want. Like his mother, Douglas also stubbornly refused to see my brother. But rancor was not in Philip's nature, and it was his gift to Douglas on his twenty-first birthday, an expensive sports car, that killed him. The accident happened late at night on a road between Yale and Vassar. His funeral was attended by the handsome wealthy boys and girls, his friends whom Philip had helped secure for him. The masses of white flowers, all those stunned young faces and my fading memories of Douglas's casual grace and his inscrutable gray eyes blended into elegiac poetry: *"I weep for Adonais — he is dead . . ."* But Norma, dry-eyed, steely stiff, a husk of a human being, and my brother sobbing as he lumbered down the aisle to a front pew, were real, a shocking spectacle of devastation left in the wake of warped, unbridled, failed living.

But Philip had always had the power of rapid recuperation and it was not long before he found Linda Darnell. Like Wendy Barrie, she was an actress, and it was she who would be the showiest gem in his collection. The account of the courtship reached me with all the glowing color and improbability of a page out of *The Arabian Nights*. The tale was reinforced by her flamboyant person. Unlike Norma Terry's her beauty was voluptuous, reminding me of one of Raphael's blooming peasant models before he had transformed her by his art into a vision of the Virgin. Everything about Linda was physically generous: she was tall, with full breasts, a large oval face and brown eyes, both wide and long like a detail magnified out of the general composition on a canvas. From a serene center part her dark hair fell to the massive curve of her shoulders. She was of mingled Indian and Spanish blood and effected native dress: flouncing dirndl skirts and laced bodices. Yet this healthful image was deceptive. Philip would always be

others. Although his Victorian manners did not permit the discussion of such matters, I sensed his disapproval of Linda Darnell in her present part. Philip was boisterously oblivious of this. He was wearing his old navy blue prepschool blazer with a gilt-embroidered insignia on the pocket and his face was sunburned (I suspected from an infrared lamp at the barber shop of the Waldorf Astoria), because as president of the Rheingold Breweries he had scant interest now in lazing in the country. My father, chairman of the board, had recently stepped down in favor of his son. The pool was mostly unused; in spite of Philip's attempts to tame her inside her cage Linda Darnell remained an exotic bird of passage. Now they were awaiting the hour to leave for the airport to receive the baby, who was being delivered to them a few days after her secret, illegitimate birth in Mexico City. Philip was excited and kept glancing at his Cartier wristwatch, but Linda appeared unconcerned, as though she were awaiting the delivery of a tin of high-grade caviar. I could not suppress a vision of the newborn infant, carefully wrapped, preserved in the ice compartment of the New York City–bound plane.

"We have decided to name her Charlotte," my brother was saying. This was after his paternal grandfather, Charles.

My father made no response. I knew this honor was distasteful to him. His heirs should be of his own flesh and blood, like my son, and not the accidental product of the coupling of two strangers. The swaddled bundle winging its way toward us was to him an unseemly acquisition, but no more so than countless other demands made by Philip to all of which my father invariably eventually capitulated.

"I do hope she is pretty," Philip said. "Her background is English, Irish and Dutch, so she will probably be a

drawn to "damsels in distress." It was his pleasure to console them for their past sorrows and so Linda Darnell, no less than Norma Terry, was a wounded soul. The nature of her injury, however, always remained a mystery. It was rumored that she had an inoperable obstruction that made normal sexual intercourse impossible, that she was a lesbian, frigid, warped by some primitive guilty Catholic inhibition — to all of which her appearance gave the lie.

I do not know how or where Philip met her. Was she discovered like Wendy Barrie years before, in the pages of some movie magazine? Did they meet in Hollywood? — by this time he had opened a southern California branch of the brewery. Perhaps it was at the home of mutual friends in New Mexico, because it was there that his picaresque wooing took place. Like Norma, like the disdainful princesses of old, Linda Darnell had demurred, and to demonstrate his ardor, I have been told (perhaps it is apocryphal), Philip hired a plane and dropped jewels down from the sky around the house in Roswell where the object of his obsession was staying. In my mind's eye I see rubies, sapphires and emeralds, a fabulous mineral hailstorm, falling in flashing red, blue and green pellets over the dun desert earth of New Mexico. But even this moneymade freak of nature apparently left her unmoved. And Don Quixote, not yet finally divorced from Norma Terry, took it into his head that, still a married man, he was compromising the fair Linda by his attentions. In his fever for an immediate settlement he signed away enough money to cripple him in his ups as well as his downs for the rest of his days. Norma's lawyers secured for her this prestigious bank account, a harsh residual life, the only kind of which she was now capable. The divorce was quickly granted and the knight returned from the joust with his prize.

Incongruously, he brought her straight to his suburban

family home in Rye, empty now of the embittered ghost of Norma Terry, the fading Rockwell Kent image of her son, the calico cat and Carmencita, the dog. But the handsome Georgian façade remained unchanged, the cabbage-rose chintz drawing room only slightly faded. The elegant oval dining room, the curving stairway with its window bench and the snug den presided over by the portrait of the stern ancestor waited to receive a new mistress. And it was to the house in Rye that we set out, my husband, my father and I, once again joined by the news of another marriage.

My pictures of Linda Darnell are few, as my encounters with my brother were rare. The marriage lasted only two or three years, and she was away during a large part of that time on location for films in many parts of the world. I retain glimpses of her in the winter at Sunday family lunches at my father's apartment in New York City. Arriving at table late, still in bedroom negligee, with her pet marmoset nestled in the capacious hollow of her shoulder, she would be sipping from a tall glass of gin while awaiting a business call from Rome, Hollywood, London, Istanbul or Cairo.

One New Year's Eve stands out in memory with the surrealist clarity of that snapshot of my brother and me behind the *trompe l'oeil* photographer's airplane. I no longer remember how my husband and I happened to be spending that night in the company of Linda and Philip, but I recall her, already half drunk, insisting on buying me a trousseau of Mexican dirndls. We are upstairs in the disorder of her bedroom, the same in which Norma Terry had once lived in ascetic neatness with the equipment for her daily make-up ranged with the precision of vials in a pharmacy. Now gaudy skirts and billowing peasant blouses were scattered everywhere. And Linda was crouching at my feet pinning and tucking. She measured my bosom, waist and hips, and

I could not help feeling like a grocery pear about to be outfitted in the gorgeous inappropriate skin of a pomegranate from some forbidden Garden of Eden. My husband and I left before midnight accompanied by promises from Linda for the prompt delivery of my new wardrobe. By this time she was extravagantly drunk and I heard that after our departure she turned with violence on Philip. I can imagine him, humble, placating and cowering while she, part Carmen, part Fury, pursued him brandishing an ordinary kitchen knife. The scenario ends here: Philip survived, Linda flew to Mexico, a new year began and my dirndl trousseau never materialized.

My last memory of Linda is on a July evening when she and Philip were awaiting the arrival of the newborn Charlotte. Like figures in a Chekhov play I see us grouped on the flagstone terrace of my brother's house: my husband and I, my father, Philip and Linda Darnell. No one spoke much except Philip, who was irrepressible. But our few commonplace words have acquired with the passage of time an undercurrent of dramatic significance. The set is the pretty trim garden separated from the terrace by a white balustrade, the backdrop is the house with its dark green shuttered windows, the time is dusk, the props the wrought-iron terrace furniture. The garden umbrella is furled before the sinking sun. The perennial philosophic Chekhovian doctor-friend is missing, so my father will play that role. He looked the part with his homely face, small wise green eyes and dapper country squire clothes. As always he seemed unrelated to his gigantic sprawling son, whom he regarded with a blend of exasperation and pride. His attitude to Linda Darnell was mixed also: always a gallant appraiser of beautiful women, his worldly code winnowed out the wives from the mistresses, actresses and

blonde." I knew he was picturing the contrasting beauty, Gypsy and Nordic, of his wife and his daughter-to-be, as though they were two works of art in a collector's showcase.

At last it was time to leave for the airport, Philip stumbling over the threshold in his clumsy eagerness, Linda rising slowly, following indolently in his wake. She would be obliged to postpone further acquaintance with her daughter as she was leaving the next day to make a film in Rome.

I believe her exit that night was her final one for me. I cannot remember seeing her again and I learned that upon her return from Rome, the marriage having grown even more precarious, she decided not to sign the adoption papers. I could imagine Philip's pleas: "But she is ours!" And I could hear Linda's retort, irritated and bored: "Send her back, I have changed my mind" — as though the shipment of caviar were an error and returnable to the delicacy shop from which it came.

But it was Linda who disappeared soon after this; Charlotte was not to be returned. Though she lacked formal sanction, she nevertheless became a member of the family. With only my brother to love her, more like a kitten than a human being, she took up her abode in the house in Rye attended by a nannie in starched white. She stopped over at my father's city apartment when Philip was away on business trips in Europe or California. For his son's sake my father overcame his disapproval and the fair sturdy baby and her nurse became intermittently part of his entourage. Motherless, tended by her two men inexperienced in the rearing of little girls, Charlotte reminded me of "The Luck of Roaring Camp" transported to Park Avenue. In the country, she waited in the newly appointed nursery (once Douglas Smith's room) for Philip's next choice. Madge Brennan was not long in arriving, Charlotte was duly legitimized and once again the enduring brick house became home base to yet another family group.

The tennis court, conspicuous to my reluctant gaze these days, was built (naturally of the most expensive material) for Madge, the third captive of the home in Rye. She was the one who endured there longest, fifteen stormy years, and it was for her to close its eyes in a kind of death when the house was sold.

What do I know of Madge? She was the least spectacular of Philip's wives and therefore the most difficult to define from my slight relationship. She was in her twenties and Philip almost forty when they married and she appeared a large bouncing outdoor type from Santa Monica who would perhaps cause less trouble than her predecessors. She was, however, pathologically shy and had married Philip in the belief that he was an important beer baron, heir to all the sophistication of New York City. But just as a pregnant woman with a whim for some out-of-season fruit, a bunch of muscatel grapes or *fraises des bois* in winter, turns away with nausea at the first taste, so now Madge was too frightened to avail herself of the benefits she had once coveted. She could be found on the tennis court early and late, vigorously exorcising her conflicts and frustrations. And Philip, still partial to emotional cripples, made matters worse by his deceptive fatherliness, calling her his "Baby Madge." A dependent himself, he delighted in turning his women into helpless children or playthings just as Circe transformed her shipwrecked sailors into swine. So there was Baby Madge to spoil as well as Baby Charlotte, along with an apricot poodle puppy and a new complement of kittens. But there were to be no others, because despite her buxom body Madge was barren and Charlotte, the rejected purchase of Linda Darnell, was received by Madge as a welcome gift.

I never knew whether Philip was aware of it or not, but although she had only average good looks, Madge bore a striking resemblance to Linda Darnell. Her proportions, her coloring, the quality of her glossy dark hair were the same. But it was as though she were reflected in a Coney Island mirror that, instead of distorting, muted the surplus beauty of the movie star into the image of an ordinary American girl. I always believed that Philip's choice of Madge was directed by his stubbornness. A failure over and over again, he would never bow to defeat, and the departed Linda was not only replaced by Madge, but physically she duplicated her, in the rough, as well.

Once again Philip, the wistful water boy of the school team, took vicarious pride in the athletic prowess of his new family. On weekends, wearing Bermuda shorts, from which his long shapeless legs emerged like stilts, he would awkwardly, with caution, descend the steep jagged stone steps to the tennis court to cheer on his Baby Madge. In a short flaring white dress with her hair tied back by a string of scarlet yarn, she looked her best. But she addressed the ball with the ferocity of a soldier confronting the enemy. It occurred to me that her true foe might be the doting debilitating love of her husband that had arrested her with no escape in a condition of insecure infantilism. As for the pool, it was alive again with splashing children as Baby Charlotte performed wonders from the diving board while Philip on the sidelines boasted with such blatancy as to cause even a five-year-old to blush. But Charlotte's star performance came later. When she was seven, Philip presented her with a pony and it was not long before, modishly dressed in a tiny crash derby, white stock and beige jodhpurs, she was winning blue ribbons in obedience and jumping classes in county horse shows. I am certain that this did more to finally seal the abdominal equestrian's wound received by my brother in childhood than the stitching, long ago, of the doctor in White Plains.

During the years Madge did nothing to alter the house. It remained as it had been in Norma Terry's time. As for Linda Darnell, I do not believe that those fabulous unreal eyes had ever seen it. Besides, my brother, in spite of the violent swings in his life, had always hated change. Sameness in his surroundings brought him comfort and the outward aspect of continuity. The only additions were numerous gilt-framed oil paintings, the works of Madge's grandmother who, in her day, had been a successful portrait painter. Her legacy to her granddaughter now hung on the walls of Philip's home, replacing a dingy landscape in the drawing room and vying with the earnest grandfather in the den. All the paintings (including one of Madge's mother as a girl) were the same: identical bygone beauties encumbered by baskets of fruits or posies. The feminine subjects, youthful, even frivolous, were depicted in somber tones that would have accorded with the heavy plushes and swag draperies of a Victorian town house. Madge was rather proud of them, attesting to a distant past more genteel than her recent one had been. But Philip was delighted by a mother-and-daughter portrait he had commissioned for Madge's birthday when Charlotte was about ten years old. Strangely, in this portrayal they looked alike: both just missed being pretty but managed to be pleasing just the same. But for Philip they were raving beauties and he exulted in their contrast — dark and fair, Snow White and Rose Red — as though they were prize flowers from his garden.

During this period Philip's crowded life and mine took differing directions and my childhood shame faded as he became merely a large hazy shape on the horizon of my consciousness. But in his amiable obtuse fashion, he would insist (the reports reaching me through mutual contacts), "My sister and I have always been very close!" Our aging father was the link between us — as were our houses, disparate but geographically close. In the summer I passed his entrance almost daily.

The last summer of my father's life, when he was too ill to travel, Philip and Madge offered their downstairs guest room as a refuge from the city's heat. He was welcomed by Madge, warm-hearted despite her violent temper, and by Philip, as prodigal in his devotion as in his selfishness. At this time my brother's extravagance had grown uncontrollable, expanding the brewery and his personal mode of existence to such a degree that both were in peril. My father watched helplessly, while Philip stretched out long tentacles like a lethal plant that would eventually strangle all the living things within its reach. Ensconced in the ground floor bedroom, my father was pathetic. Shrunken by age, he was like an old gardener incapable of saving himself from the horticultural monstrosity that he had nurtured and admired through so many years. The room was painted green, trees and shrubs crowded against the windows blotting out the sun — it was as damp and dark as a cellar. To me it suggested a tropical grave. Before the summer was spent, my father broke out of it. He preferred to return to his New York City apartment and the broiling streets, accompanied by his faithful, devoted chauffeur-valet, never to return to the house in Rye.

After my father's death several pieces of furniture salvaged from his home found their way to my brother's. One was a massive breakfront bookcase with glass doors; the volumes that had once filled it having disappeared, it now contained odd pieces of china and bibelots, like an untenanted luxury apartment that had seen better days. There was also my mother's mahogany dressing table and a familiar green glass inkwell with a silver lid purchased in London by my parents on their honeymoon. These objects contained their mute histories and in their new abode they stood out like survivors from another age.

The brewery declined as my brother, unchecked, increased his reckless spending, and eventually it had to be sold. For Philip this was a cruel severance. The golden flow of beer, his reassuring inheritance extending back over a century to the little town of Ludwigsburg, now belonged to strangers. And he never ceased to mourn it or to reassert his sentimental connection with his ancestors, the founders, those solid, practical industrious burghers, so unlike him. Despite reduced means my brother's life-style went on, and under his guidance Baby Madge and Baby Charlotte visited all the luxury spots of Europe. He maintained an unreduced staff of servitors, including a chauffeur to drive his Cadillac and a masseur who arrived in the house in Rye every evening to knead and pummel his master's passive loose-jointed body.

My brother was not hopeless about starting a new career. Nor after two failed marriages did the occasional furtive contemptuous glances of Baby Madge discourage him.

Aided by the fame of the vanished dynasty of Miss Rheingolds, my brother at fifty entered the world of advertising. Now, when my husband and I occasionally dined at his house, we found a cast of characters chosen from the large agency that employed him. This singularly vulgar world has its own laws, class system and rewards. At Philip's house I met the president: a pretentious man, careworn and pale, fresh air was for him an unknown element. Abandoning family life, with no time for recreation, he flew from city to city, from one board meeting to another. Philip, an ex-king of beer, now a minor bureaucrat on a modest salary, fawned on his chief with all the obsequiousness of a feudal nature. I also met the "artists" of this world: writers who composed catchy slogans and graphic geniuses who created the images that would snare the public into purchasing this brand rather than that.

At these gatherings I detected the first signs of shabbiness in the Rye house. The white paint on the wrought-iron terrace furniture was chipped, the chintz was definitely worn as well as faded. Only the oval dining room was still splendid, with its English china, cut crystal and multicourse dinners endured by Madge with more good nature than Norma Terry but with equal discomfort. As the evening wore on she would become increasingly silent while Philip, always the genial host, covered her withdrawal with his amiability. He would lead his guests up to the portrait of Madge and Charlotte, bright in the faded drawing room and, like one of his advertisements, more showy than the product it represented. The painted Madge dominated the room, while the real one, in her modish hostess pajamas, subsided into flushed inconspicuousness.

As time passed my meetings with Philip grew rarer and they took place mainly for the purpose of his "borrowing" money. His salary could not cover his debts but like an unbridled horse his spending galloped on. He still commuted to the city in his chauffeur-driven car and at the horse shows continued to applaud Charlotte mounted on her thoroughbred. And always there were the grand projects for the future. "I am not at liberty to tell you now," he would say, "but if a certain deal comes through it will be a matter of millions and I can assure you a huge interest on your loan — " The promise was a familiar one to which my husband and I had learned to give no heed. Even if some transaction should be realized I knew that the money would be squandered at once, the debt remaining unchanged. Incoming funds could never be more than rivulets feeding the mighty torrent of his expenses. But like my father before me, I capitulated while trying to resist, just as in a game of tug of war the weaker side falls down and relinquishes with relief the abrasive rope to the victor.

The last time I saw my brother upright, on his feet, unaided, was on a Sunday morning in early autumn. He arrived at our house after church dressed in his blue school blazer. I noticed that there were loose threads on the insignia on the pocket and the gold was tarnished. His face was red from the sun lamp at the barber shop, his tall frame more than usually stooped as he haltingly crossed the threshold of our door. And though his manner was as courtly and cheerful as ever, the frightened expression in his green gold-flecked eyes reminded me of his childhood when he had been set upon, bullied and tortured by the other boys. After polite inquiries about our families, genuine interest on his part, perfunctory on mine, he blurted out, "The bank is threatening to take my house away if I don't pay the mortgage at once — " If we would advance him the amount due he would repay it soon with ample interest. He was putting together a deal which couldn't fail to make him a millionaire many times over. He was under oath not to breathe a word about it but we would read about it in the papers any day now. With relief I watched him leave, our check in his pocket. He waved a jaunty goodby with profuse thanks and assurances that he and Baby Charlotte would include us in their prayers in church the following Sunday.

But before another Sunday came around again Philip had

been felled, cut down like a gigantic ailing elm that, towering over all the other trees around it, had menaced them with its incurable blight. The stroke occurred one evening in the Rye post office where he had gone to mail an overdue check to Norma Terry, whose lawyers had been threatening him. I could see him sprawled helpless, speechless on the cold stone floor and brought to bay at last by his pursuers.

He never lived in the house in Rye again. During two years he served time in a hospital, a rehabilitation center and nursing home. Though paralyzed on one side, with thickened speech and injured brain he continued to hope for his deals. The big one hinted at did in fact make its appearance in the newspapers, but he received no remuneration. Had he remained at his post, increased prestige would have been his only reward. Sitting by the side of the high hospital bed I helped him compose a letter to the president — the same whose pale careworn face I remembered from the dinner party at my brother's house. He was still traveling from city to city, joyless and self-important — and pitiless, for he never answered the plea addressed to him by my brother at the cost of so much effort and without a trace of rancor.

But Philip was not to be put down. Seated in his wheelchair surrounded by dotty old ladies in the nursing home, he received a business syndicate who were planning to take over a defunct brewery in Detroit. With tears in his eyes my brother told me that when he was wheeled through the plant the workers cheered him as though he were a restored monarch. But I imagined that the familiar nourishing, meaty smell of malt in the brewhouse must have been as welcome to his nostrils as the aroma of home cooking is to a traveling salesman after the synthetic fare of cafeterias and drugstores and the loneliness of the road. But most of the time my brother's conversation was concerned with the sluggishness of his bowels. Just as a wife who knows her husband is unfaithful complains only about his untidiness at home, Philip concentrated on his intestines in order to hide from himself the approach of death. He was anxious also about Baby Madge. Who would take care of her? My husband and I took over his expenses and once again in his new thick voice I heard the old refrain, "When the deal goes through, it will make us all rich — " He hoped to the end but I never knew what finally happened to the brewery in Detroit. On looking back, I now believe that the "group" was composed of shady entrepreneurs who had seized upon my brother's good name in brewing circles as a disguise, caring nothing for his pitifully maimed person, which was as expendable as an old puppet.

Philip entered the house in Rye for the last time on a hot July day; the occasion was Charlotte's sixteenth birthday. Madge had called to invite me to join them for tea. The house was for sale but no buyers had turned up yet and Philip's wife and daughter lived on there as caretakers of a haunted past. We sat in the suffocating heat of the den along with Charlotte's latest boyfriend. The upholstery was now in shreds, the leather chairs rent by gaping wounds. Philip was placed on the old sofa that had been covered by gray sacking like a shroud. Only he managed to be cheerful — as soon as the Detroit brewery was purchased and he was made chairman of the board, he would take the house off the market. By then he would be well again and Baby Madge, Baby Charlotte, the decrepit apricot poodle and the cats would resume life as before. He seemed to have forgotten that he and Madge had been on the verge of divorce before his stroke and that she had refused to take him in when he had been discharged from the rehabilitation center. True, she had visited him daily in all his hideous incarcerations and Charlotte, too, lovingly. We were now like faithful camp followers moving from barracks to barracks until forced to fall back before the front line. One Christmas, when he was still at the rehabilitation center, Madge brought him a shopping bag filled with ten-cent-store trinkets and a clear plastic block with inserted colored family photographs of another holiday season. Next to an elaborate Christmas tree Philip, Madge and Charlotte appeared looking handsome and jolly, surrounded by pyramids of costly gifts. This object remained on his bedside table in all the institutions to the day of his death. It reminded me of a fortuneteller's crystal ball, reflecting in detail a fabulous past rather than foretelling some indistinct future. Another survivor was a poinsettia plant. Having shed its spiky red petals it remained in the sickroom, a bare tough stalk supporting a few leaves in a pot covered by tinfoil. On my visits I would sometimes meet the faithful from Philip's past as well as recent friends, fellow citizens from the world of advertising. I recall, in particular, Jeff Logan, handsome and vigorous with curly dark red hair. He could lift Philip from his bed with the ease and tenderness of a nurse handling an infant. When I ran into him in the halls he would often assure me that my brother was a business genius. And I experienced again that mixture of relief and dismay known to me from long ago. Dr. Frederick Brock was another camp follower, square, serious, bespectacled. A market analyst, he was the academic of advertising. I listened as he and Philip spoke an esoteric language incomprehensible to my ears. There were also former business friends and employees from Rheingold days gathered around my brother's wheelchair during visitor's hours. I took pride in their number.

That July afternoon in the decaying den Philip was demanding another slice of birthday cake, forbidden fare as he was a diabetic and his doctors believed that this disease, which he had ignored for years from fear, gluttony and stubbornness, had caused the fatal stroke. Holding the fork in his functioning hand and lowering his gaunt putty-colored face toward the plate he ate greedily. "Your Bow-Wow loves chocolate cake," he said, addressing Madge. This revolting baby talk always set my nerves on edge; it was even more disgusting than the retching noises in the next room, remembered from childhood. But Madge appeared impervious, accepting it as she did the ridiculous prefix to her own name. As he continued to boast of the improvement in his health and the progress of the mythical deal no one dared to catch anyone else's eye. Charlotte was subdued because her horse had just been sold, Madge was overwhelmed by bill collectors and her imprisonment in the disintegrating house with its leaking roof, broken plumbing, loose plaster and the neglected tennis court and scummy swimming pool. And I, filled with pity, fretting at the bonds attaching me to this wreck in a red-and-white-check open-necked sport shirt and hospital slacks many sizes too wide for his long, wasted shanks, viewed the birthday party as I would the scene of a violent accident. Only Charlotte's friend was able to keep up with Philip's cheerful chatter. The house in Rye had no history for him. It was just old and shabby, while Charlotte was young, pretty and desirable. When the hour for his return to the nursing home arrived, Philip refused the wheelchair and, supported on one side by Madge and on the other by Charlotte's friend, he was dragged through the door, his brace squeaking, his paralyzed arm in a sling, assuring us of his speedy return.

In February Madge finally succeeded in selling the house and she and Charlotte moved with some of the now-oversized furniture into a cramped apartment in Rye. The severe grandfather now hangs in my house. I wonder what has become of all the portraits of those chubby, frilled, Victorian girls. I have also inherited a batch of old family photographs, ancestors, homely and with names unknown — along with the airplane snapshot of my brother and me and a picture of my father and Philip on their horses about to start on a morning ride. They look pleased and static as though the day had been arrested for all time at that moment. I would have wished for them a different fate. But perhaps if I were empowered to rewrite the scenario it would turn out to be a reenactment of the events that life was storing with such trickiness behind the opaque screen of the future. For sentimental reasons I rescued from my brother's house the glass inkwell with the silver top purchased on my parents' honeymoon. It is obsolete and useless, surrounded by cheap stationery-store fountain pens. And the fact that I can still recall my father's small Gothic script and my mother's round handwriting and see them dipping into that well of ink makes me feel ancient too, as though I were my own ancestor.

Madge and Charlotte gained nothing from the sale. It did not even cover Philip's debts nor pay for the accumulation of back taxes. But at last the house was gone: Philip's life line, the place to which he had always brought his new starts. And, severed from his familiar mooring, he died. It was ironic that he who had worshiped luxury with such fidelity all his life should meet his end in a room more stripped than a monk's cell, containing a tin filing cabinet for a bureau and one hospital chair. On my final visit he could barely rouse himself to respond to my forced monologue. His eyes were fixed straight ahead on a shining brass plaque inscribed to his honor by the American Brewers Association. I believe that this was the last object he saw in this world.

His funeral was large, held in the local Catholic church he had attended. As in a dream I observed figures appearing from a submerged past: pilgrims straggling out of an obliterating fog. There was Ben, our good-looking underprivileged cousin and childhood traveling companion, now a prosperous lawyer grown old and withered; Teddy Bemberg, heir to the South American tycoons once associated with the brewery; several former secretaries, forgotten friends, business colleagues and family retainers. Of course all the camp followers were present. Jeff Logan, accompanied by his pretty ex-airline stewardess wife, looked different, as though he were wearing his grief like formal attire. Before the service everyone congregated in an antichamber with the open coffin. It was my first sight of a corpse and I was grateful to a strange woman kneeling before it, hiding it from my view. I choked on the heavy scent of flowers dying in the airless room. At last the woman rose and, making the sign of the cross, moved off. My brother was revealed to me. He was covered to the waist and laid out in his old blue school blazer. His face with all care and illness expunged looked youthful. Even the large pale birthmark, his stigmata, on the high bridge of his nose, had been obliterated through the skill of the undertaker's art. His eyelids were smooth and innocent. Here in place of my brother was a knight, not a picaresque Don Quixote — but a handsome Lancelot I had never known. Suddenly I was engulfed by a wave of regret, a feeling of irretrievable waste. My brother was gone. Who was he? This question would always remain unanswered.

Today, for the first time, I passed the house without averting my eyes. The painful meaning it had for me is being rubbed out by the passing of time. Soon it will be just another suburban home indistinguishable from its neighbors.

The Dream

*A*fter the foghorn had sounded everyone knew that the cruise had begun. But the familiar sensations of sailing were not there. The motors of the QE 2 caused no vibration or noise and there was no steady swish of intercepted waves or any sea smell. It was impossible to tell whether the ship was moving forward, backward or if it were standing still.

In their cabin, the Newmans, Ben and Delphine, were unpacking their Vuitton luggage. Ben, never separated from his lawyer's briefcase, was stowing it away in a commodious concealed drawer, Delphine was hanging her unnecessary mink inside the chrome- and teak-lined closet. In spite of the deep-freeze chill of the stateroom she was suffocating — her thyroid must be acting up again. Perspiration started between her heavy breasts. She looked at Ben, but his almond-shaped gold-colored eyes were as impassive as usual and he seemed cool in his heavy dark banker's pin-striped suit. "For God's sake, put on something less funereal," she snapped and ran to the porthole. But it was sealed and blacked out. "Ring for the steward," Delphine panted. At once, noiselessly, automatically, the steward appeared in the doorway, slender and stylish in his navy blue and brass Cunard uniform. Servile, but with familiar insolence in his dark stare, he bowed slightly. And in a high-pitched nasal voice with a clipped accent, more Eastern European than British, he said, "I am Leopold Litvak, your steward. What may I do for you?"

"Open the porthole at once," ordered Delphine.

"I very much regret, madam," Litvak answered, "but all the portholes will remain locked on this cruise. You will get plenty of air through the conditioning vents. At your service, sir, madam — " Like an apparition he disappeared as suddenly as he arrived.

"I can't stand it in here. I'm going up on deck for a whiff of natural air," Delphine said.

On leaving the cabin she was confronted by an infinity of mazelike corridors, heavily carpeted, twilit. No one was about, but Delphine was comforted by the thought that behind all those doors other young millionaires' wives were managing to breathe in cabins similar to hers, with the same refrigeration system syphoning its chemical blast and the porthole boarded as tightly shut as hers. But how to reach the promenade deck — perhaps they were passing the Statue of Liberty, a landmark she remembered from childhood voyages. The sight of it would reassure her that everything was as it used to be. After all, she reminded herself, she was Mrs. Benjamin Newman, wife of the president of a successful legal-counseling firm, and this was a luxury cruise exclusively for the very rich and successful — but her feeling of helplessness persisted as she fled down one long corridor after another, without finding a way to the upper region. She thought she might scream but something told her she would not be heard.

At last she came upon the steel door of an elevator. It opened to admit her and shut at once, silently, heavily. From a hidden source, the canned cheery strains of a popular tune were a senseless accompaniment to the claustrophobia that seized her after the terror of those endless corridors. The door opened *again, a signal flashed, "Main Deck," and Delphine escaped.*

*She found herself once more amidst the plush elephantine fur-
niture and the flaming poinsettia plants of the lounges. But
there was no sign of a deck nor any opening from which to
glimpse a piece of sea or sky. She blundered through game
room after game room, past one poison green billiard table after
another, roulette wheel following roulette wheel. Television
sets were stationed at intervals to monitor this gigantic amuse-
ment world, like a palace of mechanized mirrors forever reflecting itself. Delphine darted from end to end like a trapped insect. Why was no one aboard?*

*All at once she spotted a lone figure on a television screen.
He was miles away in the farthest lounge. As she approached
him she noted that he was dressed all in black, in tight black
pants and a black turtleneck sweater. He looked like a fencer
and pinned to his chest over the region of his heart was a plastic badge like a scarlet bull's eye that read: "Leopold Litvak —
Cruise Director."*

"Where are the decks?" Delphine shouted.

*"There are no decks on the QE 2," he answered quietly.
"But everyone on board will be too busy with indoor games to
notice this small lack." His voice reminded Delphine of someone else — nasal, high-pitched with that indefinable accent.
His black eyes were boring into her; they seemed to melt her
white corpulence as though it were as unsubstantial as a mer-
ingue. "Look at all the gambling tables," the cruise director
continued, "and we have famous entertainers on board, the latest films — a thousand ways to kill time — a veritable floating
Las Vegas."*

"I want to see the Statue of Liberty," Delphine insisted.

*But Leopold Litvak, cruise director, had dematerialized and
the television monitoring screen on which she had first spotted
him showed her nothing but her own image alone in the weirdly*

deserted lounges. "This is no cruise. It's nothing but a bad dream," she said aloud. "I must have Ben get our money back — he could even start a lawsuit if necessary —" But there was no one to answer her.

SUMMER RENTALS

AFTER THE SALE of our Georgian brick home in White Plains my family rented houses in Westchester for time spared from our vacation travels abroad. While the sameness of winters blends into one long season composed of school, Central Park and the geography of a city apartment, summers remain distinct, each rental a yardstick marking another stage in growing up.

Today I often pass the first of these abodes on my route to market at a nearby farm. I have even attempted to enter the driveway but a noisy police dog bars my passage and I must be satisfied with the view from the road. Perhaps it is just as well. Closer inspection would not restore the house; its architecture has been distorted in memory so that reality has become a dream. Here is the same concrete mass, in an imitation of stone, a crude copy of the Petit Trianon palace, but now it is one solid gray color, while in recollection, three sides are that elephant hide hue with molting patches where the paint peels, and the façade on the road is strawberry mousse pink — the owner having been too stingy for more extensive repair. The door is guarded by tall neoclassical columns but they have changed positions: now they appear at the side instead of the front. Of course, the grass is paler, the old trees more commonplace and I catch no glimpse of the croquet wickets that should be planted on the lawn.

That summer we were joined by my mother's cousin, a "poor relative" and a divorcée, whose perpetual high spirits reversed her situation, causing her to appear as benefactress and my mother as the grateful recipient. Cousin Inez was the director of a theater school in New York City. She was homely, squat and swarthy and she used to say that she resembled Savonarola. Her only child, Gladys, born after years of uncongenial marriage, was blue-eyed, rosy-cheeked, buxom and ordinary, but to her parent she was a rare jewel. Cousin Inez could never take for granted the miracle of her delayed motherhood, while she felt quite at home among the modern dancers, the declaimers and assorted stage artists of her theater school. She spoke with an affected English accent, sniffing through her long hook nose and eloquently rolling her bulging brown eyes.

Our family tournaments of croquet were enlivened by her antics. Gladys and I challenged our elders; my mother would address the ball earnestly, conscientious even at play, but Cousin Inez often threw down her mallet with mock drama, insouciantly disrupting the match. And, in memory, three bending figures, an arcade of wire wickets, striped stakes like barber poles, Cousin Inez's Hannah Batik blouse, a close-up of shrill green grass studded with clover have come together to compose a kaleidoscopic design: a magnified moment rescued out of the past.

I believe the elephant gray, strawberry pink Petit Trianon was unsubstantially furnished, in keeping with the parsimony of the crabby widower who owned it. The house had high chambers with wicker chairs and tables, so flimsy that they skittered over the bare floors in a summer breeze. Cousin Inez had named the place "Windy Corners," and I have a vision of my mother and Inez (using extravagant gestures) hilariously pursuing the furniture scattered in every direction like the fallen leaves of autumn.

For me, the heart of each borrowed house was its library. Other peoples' books: musty worn volumes of detective and children's stories, wedding-gift sets of the classics were like old clothes in an attic, dated but alluring. That summer it was the Waverley novels. I wallowed in long sunsets on Scottish moors, with cavaliers and their swooning ladies. On the terrace beneath the peeling columns, I staged a dramatization of *Kenilworth,* playing the lead, while a girl with romantic black English corkscrew curls falling down her back was the heroine. Despite her exotic theatrical connections, Gladys was assigned a humble role. Although her mother was convinced that her jewel had the soul of an artist, Gladys' interests were chiefly outdoor ones. But Cousin Inez, always prepared to turn a fact to her advantage, insisted that her daughter was a healthy influence for me, and my mother, a chronic worrier, accepted this prescription, causing me to regard the good-natured Gladys with hostility, while I steered our playtime hours away from tree climbing toward my renderings of Sir Walter Scott.

That summer Gladys was the center of a mystery that was kept from me with the scrupulousness of an adult scandal. I was humiliated by my ignorance but too proud to question the docile Gladys, who suddenly appeared as an interesting invalid. One day she had been an ordinary eleven-year-old peer, the next, unaccountably, she was set apart with flushed cheeks and a furtive look in her mild blue eyes. Cousin Inez and my mother whispered behind my back and, infuriatingly, Gladys was included in the conspiracy. I was left to wander alone, enjoying my rare solitude but feeling inferior and excluded.

It was at Genungs, the village hardware store, that my curiosity got the better of me. It was there that my mother attempted to explain the mystery. We had been walking the aisles that smelled of storage, pausing before counters untidily stacked with fly swatters, tennis balls, eggbeaters, strainers, pots and pans, mousetraps, electric fans—the camping equipment of summer tenants. My impractical mother, at ease with music and Greek verse, approached the confusion at Genung's with the respect of a tourist inside the galleries of the Louvre. In front of a display of sticky flypaper, I suddenly blurted out, "What's the matter with Gladys?" There followed a jumble of embarrassing words: " — bleeding — every month — a preparation for having babies — girls of a certain age — you, too, some day — " I regretted my inquisitiveness and bravely lied, "Oh, is that all — I know all about that — " For some time afterward it was my belief that menstruation was an affliction suffered by females of about eleven for a short period during the summer season, from which they recovered upon reaching womanhood. It somehow became linked to Genung's hardware store, its stale smell and shelves stocked with the lowly necessities of housekeeping, and to my mother's role as the temporary chatelaine of Windy Corners.

I grope to recall the next house located only a few minutes from Windy Corners, but by the compass of childhood it was a continent removed, with a different climate, topography and population. My family, mother, father, brother, reappear, but as in a traveling stock company, another year has produced a new repertory.

Situated on a slight rise of land, this house now overlooks a map of thruways. It is enclosed by a white lattice fence modestly concealing the dwelling from my prying gaze. Once I lived within and the wooden barrier repulsed our enemy, not the automobile, but invasion by microbes. It was the summer of a record-breaking epidemic of infantile paralysis, a disease that has become almost as historic as bubonic plague. Nowadays, when other people exclaim over the new threats to existence, I cannot help feeling that insecurity is a constant.

In our rented retreat all outsiders were foes. Even the milkman might be carrying contagion with his cool white bottles in their wire baskets. He must be halted at the gate. That summer my brother and I were in quarantine, seeing no one but the family next door, which included the girl with black corkscrew curls, the heroine of my *Kenilworth*. Her family was similarly confined in a summer rental, but with the ingenuity of childhood I was able to invest a visit to that home with all the exoticism of foreign travel, and I do not recall feeling like the prisoner that, in fact, I was. This house, a fake Swiss chalet, contrasted with ours and was memorable for its roof thatched in grass. When we moved from this domain to ours, we were journeying from the Alps and back home to New England. In many ways it was preferable to the real thing because we were free to travel on our own without the red tape of railroad schedules or hotel accommodations — an intricate world of adult maneuvering in which a child could participate only passively.

That season was agreeably idle. There were no projects, day camps or lessons and no swimming; the shock of cold water was said to increase susceptibility to the disease. We ran from swing to slide, from garden to shuttered rooms, and we felt safe and contented. Polio and kidnaping, the twin ogres of my childhood, were remote. But anxiety filtered through my mother's frightened expression as she read in the paper of the rising toll of the epidemic, or attempted to flatten an agile, germ-laden fly against wall or table. She, from whom I sought protection, disclosed naked dread. It was as though the lattice fence should collapse, exposing the fastness of the house to the world outside; my mother's white face seemed to be telling me that the joy of a summer day was illusory, that it also might shatter without warning.

The setting for an early love is special, idyllic, by tradition. Yet the year I was sixteen, when I met Kenneth, found me in a country house so nondescript that I can remember nothing about it but its location, adjacent to those earlier places. But once again, it was removed by the passage of time and by the miraculous event of falling in love. I dimly see white shingles and a prim rose garden with a sundial that I never bothered to consult, as my hours were indicated by the ring of a telephone and the crunch of wheels of an open roadster on a gravel driveway. The essence of that summer was contained in a popular tune: with today's nostalgia for the thirties, I sometimes hear again the strains of "These Foolish Things Remind Me of You," and through the telescope of years I see two tiny figures. I, emerged from the grub of a skinny child into a creation in a tight white Lastex bathing suit that I thought showed off becomingly my long tanned legs. My face displeased me, lacking my mother's classically chiseled features and her fair beauty, but I emphasized my differences in the hope that I might look like a dashing Latin type, a femme fatale, while my self-confidence remained as wobbly as Jell-O. Kenneth, the other figure, seemed perfect. At seventeen, he had for me the understated sex appeal of the current British matinee idol, Leslie Howard. He was the scion of an immensely rich Jewish merchant family, but several generations of money had converted them to a flawless semblance of English gentry. Shadings of privilege may sometimes be contrasted, and in those days, Jewish society was divided into ranks now extinct, but accepted then with the blindness of insular snobbery. My family was located in the middle. Third-generation Americans, habituated to every comfort at home, we were, nonetheless, European-oriented. Beneath us were the immigrant Russians and Poles, and above were the lordly rich, Kenneth's world. He could expertly handle rod, reel and gun, all neglected in our education.

I observed his home in detail because it was the setting for him and, also, because with adolescence I had lost my pleasure in exploring a new country house each season and I envied those who were aristocratically rooted in their own suburban soil. His parents were the proprietors of an English castle, imported stone by stone. I marveled at the extensive acreage of Gray Turrets: its formal flower gardens, maze of clipped box hedge, paddocks, greenhouses tended by a resident army of employees. At the swimming pool I was not offended by the spectacle of Kenneth's older brother reclining on a rubber raft — a frog on a lily pad — while a butler served him iced drinks from the shore. The only shadow on the scene was Kenneth's mother, who was confined by a mysterious illness to her bedroom. I saw her just once when she appeared in an upstairs window calling down to her son. Her blond frizzy hair, haggard face and shrill voice reminded me of tenement women I had seen leaning on their sills, glimpsed in passing as a train emerged from the sooty darkness of Grand Central tunnel.

Kenneth and I often visited the stables of Gray Turrets, where I admired the blooded hunters with their glossy haunches. I could recapture there the picture of Kenneth mounted high on his steed, booted and spurred, riding in the county horse shows. He cleared the jumps easily, coattails flapping behind him like wings, his number pinned to his back like a badge of victory, his seat on his horse so firm that no space ever showed between his body and the saddle, as, centaurlike, he rose into the air. Worshipfully, I compared his performance with my own at a neighborhood riding academy where I had been taking lessons for several years. I had begun in a damp indoor ring in which the sod was soft as a padded pillow. I would prod my spiritless rented beast into a reluctant canter, bumping up and down on the saddle while Mr. Carrol, the instructor, bellowed instructions from the sidelines. I had graduated to rides in the sultry woods. Mr. Carrol and I walked the horses, our saddles creaking companionably, side by side. One season I even considered falling in love with his weather-beaten face and his aquamarine eyes beneath heavy black brows. But by the time I was ready to attempt jumping the lowest barriers in the outdoor ring, I precipitously fell out of love. The leap into the void was terrifying and intensified my distrust of the horse. I had always avoided its large perilously stupid eye when I proferred the customary lump of sugar at the end of the lesson. And my lack of confidence came to include Mr. Carrol and his harsh commands; I gave up riding. So Kenneth's skills, the blue ribbons and silver trophies he won, his Leslie Howard countenance beneath a stylish black crash derby had a special value. They were like prize possessions, always beyond my reach.

At night, inside his roadster, our fumbling experimental embraces were new and the familiar countryside, the back roads where we parked, were transformed into a bewitched landscape, dark, abstract and hushed. When he finally returned me to my house, the lights in the kitchen where we ravenously raided the icebox were a shock. He often exhibited a feat of which he was exceedingly proud. Selecting a raw egg, he would stuff it whole and unpeeled in his

canopy that was as flimsy as the construction of Kenilworth castle, made in childhood from discarded blankets and porch furniture.

My husband and I returned to the house unexpectedly, summoned by a wheezing, reedy voice over the transatlantic phone announcing the sudden death of my mother. Abruptly we abandoned our hotel room that had been a world to us during our brief stay. In the early afternoon we used to lie between damp sheets, gritty with sand imported from outside by our bodies, our skin tasted sticky with salt. Shutters closed to temper Mediterranean midday heat made an artificial evening and we seemed to be making love in a cove hidden from other humans exposed to sea, sand and our private night sky. But the unrelenting murmur of the waves failed to warn us.

After disembarking, we called on friends of my mother. The elderly childless couple received us in a town house remembered as the place for Christmas celebrations for the benefit of other peoples' children. This pair had hovered near my mother's deathbed while I had been far away in that seaside hotel. Their condolences were for an unreal woman, someone I had never met. But their house was actual, its antiques shrouded in summer dust covers. They were also the owners of a home in Connecticut, and it was as though this double proprietorship gave them permanency, a perpetuity denied my mother, who had been transplanted so many times.

My widower father awaited us in the empty house. Was it possible that only two weeks earlier it had been the scene for a wedding pageant? The return was a mockery: it was no homecoming and I was neither bride, wife nor daughter, but a changeling sprung from the metaphysical horror of sudden death. Shocked, without grief, I roamed the house:

mouth, regarding me solemnly as he crunched it shell and all. Astonishment was expected of me and I gave it generously, but I continued to prefer the sight of Kenneth, with nonchalant mastery, clearing the fences in the county horse shows, coattails flying, horse and boy as one.

Later that summer in Europe, I received several letters from him. I hated my parents for dragging me away and I feared some other girl might be wandering over the grounds of Gray Turrets, taking my place at the horse shows and inside the roadster. Perhaps he was even crunching eggs in someone else's kitchen! At the beginning of September in the Alps, my last letter from him arrived. It enclosed a newspaper photograph of movie actress Kay Francis underscored with the word, "You," and an exclamation mark. I was flattered and I studied her face, but Kenneth–Leslie Howard had already started to recede into an impersonal past, a brightly faceted instant that was not to be regained.

Now, when I meet him on rare occasions, I do not recognize a middle-aged man who resembles a bald eagle. And I am certain that he remembers less than I a certain summer which I am rescuing from the anonymous pauper's grave in which time deposits all its devalued trinkets.

As for Gray Turrets, it has become a veterans' hospital. Recently I drove through it, but I could not find the stables, swimming pool and box-hedged paths. A few old toothless ex-soldiers from forgotten wars, wearing ill-fitting khaki reclaims, were sunning themselves on institutional benches on a grass plot overgrown by weeds in front of the castle that had been imported stone by stone from England.

Meanwhile, our former house has been completely concealed among trees grown taller and fuller. The owner's name, Durand, proclaims on the gatepost the breed of rightful resident coveted in my girlhood. The road is unchanged but in a wide area surrounding it the land has been sheared to make way for one more IBM installation.

The final house, in Armonk, New York, was rented by my family for two successive summers before my marriage. It marked an end and a beginning but, perhaps, because the setting for so many changes in my life belonged to strangers, the events occurring beneath that roof do not seem real.

Again, I see white clapboard and black shutters but the garden appears more extensive. There are more rooms: an entrance hall, cool even on the hottest day, with a round, convex, gilt-framed mirror containing a distorted bosky green reflection; to the right, a den in which the wedding gifts had been laid out on long tables with inventories and tickets as in a department store; on the left, the dining room with a sunny breakfast nook, bow-windowed, cheerfully wallpapered with a pattern of flowers and birds. Upstairs a separate wing included the spacious master bedroom in which my mother died two weeks after my marriage.

The wedding was a theatrical performance, the garden festive with June flowers — late peonies, iris, delphinium and roses. The musical prelude was the familiar whirr of the lawn mower and the rhythmic ping of tennis ball hitting racket, I, the leading lady, my husband-to-be, the male star. At that time he was known to me chiefly by the lifting of my own heart, and apart from that he was a dark stranger playing opposite me in a drama so absorbing that it obliterated any memory of the past or uncertainty about the future. My mother was the amateurish stage manager, assisted by technicians. It was she who sat by my side while I was fitted inside a white satin sheath and garlanded in tulle veiling. She, usually so inattentive to worldly things,

had helped place and tag the wedding presents in the den; she plotted with the caterer, worried about the Mont Blanc cake, the candy-striped marquee, the weather. She was looking harassed and fragile, but I went through my paces unperturbed. My father had his role of low-keyed philosophical comic. The evening of the rehearsal I paraded on his arm toward the improvised altar in the garden, composed of two white plaster urns filled with summer flowers. They resembled funeral parlor accessories but I was too preoccupied to care. The ushers, a bland chorus line, arrived from all directions; the bridesmaids had no reality without their swaying organdy and flapping hats.

The day of the wedding dawned black, the morning as dark as a night that did not lift. The rain fell in a barrage, causing leaves to sigh and toss their watery load. Within our borrowed shelter, the mirror in my bedroom was the brightest object. It reflected an unaccustomed figure: a female warrior armored in satin and tulle with a delicate bouquet of scented lilies of the valley for a shield. The traditional strains of the *Lohengrin* wedding processional announced the rising curtain. Down the aisle I marched with my father, but he was not himself but that actor hired for the occasion. On either side a sea of blurred faces was the audience. Before the plaster urn my fiancé and the ushers waited: wax mannequins in correct white flannels and blue blazers with carnations in buttonholes. The bridesmaids moved ahead, as unassuming daisies in an overgrown field. The rain pelted the candy-striped tent; its flaps lowered against the deluge were ineffectual in preventing a steady leakage. I remained calm, progressing slowly in time to the music. My long train fanned behind like the path of the past moving across a rented threshold toward a makeshift altar and the future, beyond a wedding

the cool entrance hall, with its convex distorting mirror, the sunken living room, the gay breakfast nook, the den, emptied of gaudy display, it seemed, now, as though each object had been a sharp-edged lethal instrument. I refused to sleep in my former bedroom, where the mirror might give back, instead of the warrior bride, the image of a grotesquely garlanded sacrificial calf, and my husband and I lodged in the strangeness of a guest room where, when I woke in the morning, the sound of bird song seemed shrill and fraudulent.

I avoided my parents' quarters, the dangerous place where the fatal illness had occurred. I would not talk about it, but fragments penetrated my unwilling ears. Here it was that my mother, drowning internally in her own blood, had clutched at my father, her life line, pleading, "Don't let me die!" She, who had always been quiveringly alert to danger, like an electric wire in a thunderstorm, had been, at the end, caught unprepared — "Don't let me die" — a primitive cry, as raw and defenseless as an infant's wail at birth.

Her disappearance was without transition. I collected my meager memories, but they were as trivial as old letters, conserved but no longer treasured: my mother's gusts of gaiety, the spell of her conversation, her silhouette at the piano, in the compartment of a European wagon-lit — her satchel handbag crammed with the emergency equipment of a Red Cross kit — our shopping expeditions, she on the sidelines, I stage center.

Only a short time before, I had seen her for the last time through the rain-streaked window of our car as my husband and I set out on our wedding journey. She had been dressed in pearl gray and her features beneath the wide brim of her hat were ethereal, the familiar lines and anxious expression erased for the instant. Love was written across her face, but in my eagerness for the next step, I did not bother to decipher the message. The twenty years I had known her were as nothing now.

In an attempt to rescue my father with the distraction of small occupations, we began bridge lessons in the den. But like an old man he would drowse over the cards and I was unable to concentrate on the black and red symbols. The bridge lessons were disbanded; the summer over at last, my husband and I, still strangers to one another, left for the Middle West, where we were to live temporarily. The whole family had fled the house that had been witness to so much drama — a bad dream from which, in time, we would awaken.

Mountain laurel still mean Westerleigh: bushes with leaves like green patent leather and white pink-tinted blossoms. They bloomed everywhere, along the driveway, hugging the house, breaking out in the woods behind with a prodigality that imitated a full corps de ballet. When the sun slanted through the shade after rain it would strike the mountain laurel causing the pink clusters to shimmer like sequined tutus.

This flowery richness matched the house, a Colonial-style mansion leased by my father the summer following my mother's death. Perhaps, in the past, her simple taste had restrained his instinct for elegant opulence which paralleled his irrepressible zest for life. That season, he reigned, a small swarthy king at Westerleigh. But for me — who had known him only as a father — he remained a family man deprived of his mainstay — and so, forever, bereft. For this reason, I, my husband and my brother kept him company, and I retraced a childhood pattern that had grown obsolete.

Looking back, I can see that my father, at sixty-eight, had reverted to his bachelorhood. He had even said to me, with a certain wonder, "My marriage was only a small island in my life." And it was true. Eleven years my mother's senior, he was to outlive her for twenty more; the end of his existence a prolonged but diminishing encore.

From that summer, a young woman, a new friend of my father's, Leslie Ashton, remains in memory. I see her by the swimming pool, slim, blond, lily white, with the regular features he always admired, perhaps because they were so different from his own. The pool is a prototype lined in standard blue tile, with a flagstone border. It might have been the one that used to belong to Kenneth's family in which his brother floated, indolently — or, in prophecy of things to come, my brother's, where first Douglas, then Charlotte, performed like dolphins before his admiring eyes. Leslie Ashton did no more than dangle her pedicured feet in the clear water. Although she wore a modish bathing suit, the series of jangling gold bangles on her thin arm, her expensive beach equipment, fitted canvas bag, Dior scarf, sun oil and cream and her coral-enameled toenails reminded me of pictures of ladies of the Bel Epoque approaching the sea, fully dressed in veiled hats, sailor blouses, knickers and long rubber-soled stockings. I did not associate her with my father's private life nor did I resent her presence; she appeared as inanimate and uninteresting as another pool fixture.

Strangely, a painting inside the house, on the landing halfway up the grand staircase (fit for miniopera or ballroom), was more alive for me than Leslie Ashton. It was a portrait of the deceased mistress of Westerleigh in a scarlet evening gown out of the 1920s. She surveyed me with haughty black eyes that made me feel like an interloper. Also, the painted likeness represented disloyalty to my mother in a way that Leslie Ashton, an insipid, sleek copy of her, did not. It was as if the glowing dark beauty confronting me from her immovable position on the stairs was causing the already fading image of my mother to grow paler and more blurred with the passing of the days. But that summer had its end also and the portrait was buried along with the house.

It towers now, an ungainly giant, above a development of ranch-style homes. And the mountain laurel has disappeared, mowed down in the path of the bulldozer.

For over a quarter of a century, Sarosca Farm, once belonging to my husband's grandparents, has been ours. Inside the hand-built fieldstone wall the number of summers mount. But the worn, old-fashioned, accommodating house and its grounds remain unaltered. The lawn slopes toward a gazebo smothered in wisteria vines; a variety of shrubs, lovingly planted by my husband's grandfather, continues to thrive. In the vegetable garden my husband and I celebrate the seasons: fresh dangling pea pods in June, an explosion of raspberries for the Fourth of July, late summer deep, gold-tasseled corn, the hard clinging knobs of Brussels sprouts at the arrival of frost. We have watched our young son wavering down the pitted driveway on his first two-wheeler and over the same area this accomplishment has been repeated by our granddaughter. For us, Sarosca Farm, more than any other place, stands for continuity, yet I grow increasingly aware of change. Long ago my husband routed that dark stranger, the leading performer at a rainy garden wedding, a tall bearded man, my son, has no connection with the child on a new blue bicycle. And, most incredibly, I have become the replacement for the grandmother; original matriarch of Sarosca Farm, whose

venerable bulk and scanty white silken hair I recall, ensconced in her favorite armchair. It endures in its corner,
but it has become a contour seat appropriated by our large
black poodle, his head resting on one arm, his tail draped
across the other.

A generation has the span of a summer and I am forced to
concede that this house, like those resurrected from my
youth, is, after all, a rental too.

The Dream

T *he Oberdorfers and the Mellows always traveled*
together. The two couples presented a solid front with
which to approach a foreign land. Away from their
home base in Dallas, they could never be certain that their indi-
vidual status would be recognized, although American dollars
were impressive everywhere. Therefore the Mellows and the
Oberdorfers were exacting about their accommodations, taking
the best in the best hotels for granted, and invariably flying first
class. Marty Mellow, six feet tall, weighing well over two
hundred pounds, claimed he needed the leg room, but they all
knew better. On the Young Millionaires' cruise they were quite
disturbed that there was only one model luxury suite and that
had already been preempted. The Oberdorfers and the Mellows
were obliged to make do with second best.

While the other passengers ate in their cabins, they preferred
breakfast in the dining room. Marty felt he could get a more
substantial meal there. On the second morning out they found
themselves alone in the restaurant. Marty was enjoying his
usual cornflakes, fried eggs and flapjacks. The men were talking
business while the women discussed housekeeping.

Al Oberdorfer had made his fortune in the manufacture of
bombsight parts. A thorough hawk, he never ceased to lament

the loss of United States authority in Southeast Asia and to predict worse to come from the Reds. He was a mild-looking young man, tall and lanky, prematurely stooped, with a receding hairline and dreamy blue eyes. His wife, Jill, was small, homely, dark, all angles and points. But her origin was New York City and that lent her a certain distinction. By now her Texas drawl was more pronounced than that of her indigenous companions, and she was aggressively "chamber of commerce," always referring to her family in Manhattan as "those effete Easterners."

Marty Mellow was the president of one of Dallas' leading department stores. His wife, Pam, a pretty straw blonde with turquoise eyes, had been a TWA stewardess before her marriage. Although her wealth was new, her acquisitiveness was not. From her flying days she had collected trophies from every country. In the Mellow home were elephant tusks hollowed into plant stands, a sedan chair housing a telephone, silks from Persia, ashtrays from Hong Kong, bits of stone chipped off the Acropolis and the Forum, idols from India and carvings from Egypt. Marty and Pam had four children, but in his wallet he carried photographs of his house in shrill Kodachrome, snapped from every angle. Fellow voyagers were expected to exclaim over its strawberry mousse pink façade. An exact replica of the Petit Trianon, it looked smug but naked, set in an unshaded flat plot of land in a Dallas suburb.

Al, Jill and Pam were through and they were waiting for Marty to finish. With slow deliberateness he sopped up a last morsel of pancake and syrup and hailed his waiter for seconds. Leopold Litvak, the maitre d', did not appear at breakfast time — he was a night bird — and the Mellows and the Oberdorfers had already complained about the service. Also their table steward had a sinister aspect. In spite of the generous tip already bestowed upon him, his eye was hostile. "He looks like a pickpocket," Al observed, adding, "probably a Commie."

The girls were growing restless. For this there was one sure remedy: shopping. On board the QE 2 there was an arcade of stores only slightly smaller than Palm Beach's Worth Avenue. Jill and Pam wandered in and out of the boutiques, pricing, fingering, comparing and estimating. The jeweler's showcase displayed a golden frog lapel clip, studded with warts of emerald, ruby and sapphire.

"This I must have," Jill exclaimed. When she left the jeweler's with the frog secured to her spectator sports dress, her spirits rose like the barometer of a ship sailing toward fair weather.

In her cabin she removed the frog for more careful examination. It sat heavily on the palm of her hand, regarding her as though its emerald eyes were alive. All at once the chill quiet was disrupted by a violent gust of wind. She only had time to think that it reminded her of the sultry tornados back home before the jeweled frog hopped from her hand and out the porthole, suddenly torn open. The electricity went off and although the sky was somber, a blinding north white light streamed from the opening, leaving the rest of the interior in total darkness. A strong smell of salt rushed in, accompanied by the unmistakable odor of rot. Jill ran to the window but she was too overwhelmed by the loss of the frog to realize that this was her first view of the ocean since the cruise had started. Although by this time they were two days out, the sullen gray water was littered with debris of all kinds: cans, dismembered chair legs and bedposts, floating condoms that looked like withered jellyfish and a high, archaic porcelain bathtub bobbing on top of the waves like a lifeboat. But the jeweled frog had vanished. As Jill searched in vain, the wind subsided, the porthole closed and the eye was blind again. It was as though the miniature hurricane and the miniature jeweled toad had never been —

MANY MANSIONS

A NAME through habitual use clings to a person like a barnacle to a floating log, growing as much a part of him as his features or his coloring. For this reason it bothered me that my brother and Philip Rahv bore the same first name. In life I was mostly heedless of this coincidence, but as soon as I decided to commit them to paper it became an obstacle. I even considered renaming my brother, but that would have been to rob him of his birthright. These two men, so different, yet with one name, what would I do with them? Then I remembered my mother in my childhood translating our Greek names: Dorothea, "gift from God"; Philip, "lover of horses." I had been well pleased by my superior status! Now in the recall of my brother and Philip Rahv, the meaning of their name takes on new significance for my own purposes. Change one letter and, presto, "lover of horses" becomes lover of houses — the one characteristic shared by both. The performance of this small trick having established the "Philip" part of them to my satisfaction, I can proceed, confident that though names or words may be impressive in themselves they can never come close to encompassing the mystery and multiplicity of a single human equation.

I met Philip Rahv on a Saint Patrick's Day in the late 1940s at the home of Emmy and Louis Kronenberger, then theater critic for *Time* magazine. I know the date because it was the night of a record end-of-winter blizzard. Fresh snow in New York City is magic despite the subsequent filth, confusion and paralysis it causes. Silent, it hushes the general noise, obliterates time and alters space. It transforms the metropolis into the same small town we glimpsed in childhood, resurrected every time there is a heavy, soft, muted fall of snow. I can see the glistening crust close to my eyes as I lie face down on my belly while my father pulls my sled toward Central Park, redecorated in white on this Sunday morning to resemble an alpine resort. Or, it is a weekday and due to the severity of the storm all automobiles have been banned from the streets. But my husband, with the temerity of a North Pole explorer, defying nature, chooses to ignore the order. Rounding up our small son and his friends, he packs them into his car and heads for school. With his load of ski-suited, hooded, mittened, booted children eager and curious in this strange newborn world, he proceeds cautiously along the deserted streets, skidding between high white banks, the chains on his tires clanking and crunching in the unaccustomed silence. He is Admiral Byrd but he is also, partly, the homey, reassuring narrator of Thornton Wilder's play *Our Town,* and the boys and girls are the citizens of a temporary hamlet, far more exciting than the crowds and clamor of their native city. All my Christmases are joined — those of my childhood, my son's and my granddaughters' — by the presence, the anticipation or the hope of that same snowstorm appearing again and again to astound our vision and make us lose track of the passage of time.

Shelter is intensified when it snows and houses become

unusually alluring. Perhaps this is one reason I remember that particular party we went to at the Kronenbergers'. They lived on 95th Street between Lexington Avenue and Park. The block is unchanged; it has a small-town ambience and is lined with small private houses, their front doors painted bright red, green or blue. Many are high-stooped, all are solid but unstylish like prosperous shopkeepers of the neighborhood, in contrast to their more socially aristocratic peers to the south. The atmosphere is old-fashioned and snug and on that Saint Patrick's eve with the snow gaining momentum outside, the Kronenbergers' house enclosed us in warmth. The narrow entrance was already filled with discarded wraps suspended from a clothes rack rented for the occasion. Beneath it were galoshes with melting snow still clinging to them and damp umbrellas huddled like chaperones on the periphery of the party already underway in the living room and the adjoining dining room, overheated, vibrating to the multivoiced roar of a literary gathering. Many of the faces are lost to me. Perhaps this is because youth is too intent on its own image to enable it to see others clearly. At that time, on entering a crowded room, anticipation and uncertainty took possession of me and just as a traveler starting out upon a journey is caught up by the sensations of motion and change themselves and is too excited to see out of the window of the train or plane, I too was missing the fleeting scene. I do recall W. H. Auden, old even then, his face a map of lines; Lionel Trilling, writer, professor, slight and shadowy gray, with a mind as drawn to pure knowledge as is a moth to the light; his wife, Diana, the critic — and our host and hostess, he, elfin, cozy and chatty, she, diminutive, with bright black eyes. I moved among countless others making conversation, taking note of my own undeveloped skills, like a novice eager to learn the intricate steps of a gavotte.

Suddenly a presence broke through my self-absorbed blindness. He was standing at the far end of the dining room, taller and broader than everyone else. He had an oversized head with a shock of black hair, was swarthy and had a generous nose that turned up comically at the end, making it look like an implement — a sort of shovel with which to dig up the absurdities and foibles of those around him. His lips were thick but shapely and there was something poetic about their sensuality in contrast to the rest of his plebeian appearance. He looked like a truck driver set down at a gathering of college professors. Drawn to him and forgetting my diffidence, I pushed and elbowed my way to where he stood. When I drew close I observed that his large brown eyes set in dark shadowed puffs were surprisingly gentle and thoughtful yet unflinching.

I no longer remember how we started to talk, but I was hypnotized by his speech, guttural and soft, with an accent so heavy that it was all I could do to recognize a stray word here and there. Yet it was enough to convince me of his bold intelligence and a sincerity as aggressive as his physical person. I remember his talking that night — or rather lecturing — on the subject of Thomas Mann. He would emphasize his points with wide flappings of his hands interspersed by rough absent-minded nudgies at me. Who was this man with his thick foreign accent, discussing *The Magic Mountain* and *Dr. Faustus* with such brilliance while looking like a peasant recently converted to city life? Abruptly he broke off his monologue, which seemed more like a retort. Although I had not had the chance or the courage to utter more than a few words, his pronouncements were delivered with so much combativeness as to sound like violent rebuttals directed at an invisible, inaudible opposition. After a pause, in a different tone, caressing yet impersonal and blunt, he said, "You're quite pretty. What's your name?"

He did not tell me his, and, flattered and confused, I failed to ask him. The fierce literary lecture resumed. "Dey don't write anymore — dey just talk about demselves, no sense of history, no social sense, just dere own intestines. Who cares, huh? Who do dey tink dey are?" Followed by another vigorous jab at my ribs.

I spent the remainder of the evening with him, and when the party broke up I rejoined my husband, telling him about this strange man with his thick accent, brusque manner and astounding knowledge of literature and recent history. "How did he land here?" I asked. "What sort of truck driver is he?" Amazed at my ignorance, my husband answered, "He is Philip Rahv, the co-founder and editor of *Partisan Review* and a famous critic."

Afterward I remembered my first meeting with Philip and realized how characteristic of him it had been. Always aware of his ugliness, never realizing its fascination, he was nonetheless a lusty woman-taster. Yet he refused to trade on his position. "Bah," he would exclaim contemptuously, "most girls prefer ink to blood!"

At the front door, on our way out, we met again. Now he was with his wife, Nathalie, stout, florid and thoroughly drunk at this moment, but with a dignity that was impressive. She looked like an American Valkyrie dimmed by approaching middle age and a certain weariness. Philip bundled his bulk into an ulster, wound a thick woolen scarf around his neck and placed an absurdly small felt hat at a rakish angle on his large head. It looked like the lid of a kitchen pot on top of a barrel. Through the open door we confronted the cold night. The streetlamps revealed the snow, unmarred by any footprints. The level had risen rapidly while we had been inside, covering the stoops and reaching up to basement windows like a minor mountain range. Snow was still falling in large crowding flakes. Now East 95th Street looked like Moscow, but with Philip Rahv in our midst it was not the city of name-day receptions and balls but a place of intellectual and social upheaval on the eve of revolution. Far away I heard an automobile coughing its way to life out of the freeze. I was back in New York and the year was 1947. We proceeded slowly down the steep buried stoop, clinging to the wet balustrade for support. Only Nathalie in her state of aloof, regal drunkenness ignored it, and, missing the first step, down she floated. Light and buoyant as a balloon despite her heft she landed miraculously upright on her feet on the sidewalk, her immense dignity still intact. This first fantastic presentation of her remains: a lady, indestructible, proud, self-sufficient, uncommunicative and, perhaps, lonely.

After the evening at the Kronenbergers' I recall our first party at Philip and Nathalie's Greenwich Village apartment — one floor-through of an old house. The gathering had its historic aspects: it was an event that would be discussed over and over by the small group of intellectuals over which Philip presided. It was fuel for the kind of gossip that he himself relished when it was about others — but now he was center stage along with Mary McCarthy. It was a first meeting, a reconciliation after a feud lasting several years following the breakup of their early relationship, her defection by marrying Edmund Wilson, their divorce and the publication of her satiric novel on academic life, *The Oasis,* in which Philip made an unpleasant appearance. I observed Mary McCarthy. It was my first introduction to this personality with the reputation for a "cold eye," caustic tongue and sharp mind. She was sitting demurely in a rocking chair and she looked like a beautiful pioneer: brown hair parted in the center and drawn severely back into a bun at the nape of her neck, clear, wide-open gray eyes, sculptural features and good bones — she was the American equivalent of the Greek harmonies. In my mind's eye I saw her dressed in homespun cloth suitable for the labors of opening up the New Land, but in reality Mary McCarthy was engaged in making her own clearing in the small special world of New York intellectuals. An early contributor to *Partisan Review,* she had been Philip's special protégée. Now he eyed her with distrust and defiance, tinged, I thought, with a look of soft melancholy. The wounds he had suffered through her might be denied by the gruff aggression of his words but they were indelibly inscribed in his eyes. He was like a poet turned diplomat who furtively indulges his muse only after working hours, in the belief that he is unobserved. For those who knew him well, Philip was a romantic despite his self-taught hardheadedness.

He was holding forth on the "new criticism": "Why do dey try to turn de clock back? Freud, Marx and Trotsky can never be forgotten. Notting will ever be de same again." This was punctuated by the rough pokes and nudges at the person closest to hand. Philip was one of the army of disillusioned ex-communists. In the thirties he had cut his Party ties, viciously denouncing Stalin and the Soviets in his writings and in his talking. But he still clung to shreds of his abandoned faith, in the form of his own brand of Trotskyite socialism.

We sat in a circle in his sparsely furnished living room — on the floor, on cushions, stools, chairs borrowed from bedroom and kitchen. The walls were hung with crude examples of abstract expressionism by obscure artists. Philip's eyes were focused inward on cerebral matters, and it always seemed to me that he was blind to the visual world — with the great exception of women! And Nathalie was undomestic, concentrating on her architect's career. The room grew hot, the conversation strenuous. I remember Delmore Schwartz, the unhappy neurotic poet whose genius was never to be fully born; that wise woman, Hannah Arendt, a Hitler refugee and a disciple of Karl Jaspers'. Years later, Philip would differ with her over her book on the Eichmann trial. Choosing to ignore its warning against all bureaucrats for whom Eichmann was a prototype, Philip felt that she had been too mild, too lenient on the man. Philip never failed to align himself forcibly with the plight of his fellow Jews the world over. Dwight Macdonald was there, competing with Philip in audacious sallies, accompanied by high derisive laughter. But his satirical brilliance was only an interlude in the persistent tone of Philip's sardonic utterances, just as in a minor-key symphony a major theme is introduced for contrast without changing the dominant darkness of the composition.

Nathalie sat by silent and unscrutable in the midst of her noisy guests. They reminded me of actors in an old film depicting the intellectual ferment of the early days of the student rebellion in Russia, viewed in the light of the present moment, with nostalgia, but through the revealing glasses of hindsight. When it was time to leave, my husband and I excavated our coats from the pile on the Rahvs' king-size bed, a fit battlefield for the private wars of two contending giants.

During the years I knew him, Philip moved from Greenwich Village to Riverside Drive, to the East Side near

Bloomingdale's (where he liked to browse in the Gourmet Shop, always fancying himself a master chef), to a spacious studio off Central Park West. Although he remained essentially urban, a man who might have been at home at a European café surrounded by a coterie of international professors and writers, my most vivid pictures of him are set against bucolic backgrounds from which he stands out like a slow-moving hippopotamus incongruously transplanted from some faraway land into a field of American daisies, goldenrod and clover. The first portrait shows him at Bridgewater, Connecticut. The house has disappeared from my view, accompanied by other faces. It is noon of a summer's day and he is sitting by the side of an old stone well that looks like the property of a transcendental commune in the New England of Emerson and Thoreau. Philip's dark shadow extending over the grass resembles a sundial, a reminder of a somber alien past projected onto the bright light of the present hour. He is dressed in slacks and a sport shirt as loud as his avant-garde paintings and he is gazing into the well. His expression is not to be forgotten: ruminating, far-seeing and surprisingly vulnerable.

By this time I had learned something of his history — from others — as he was always stubbornly secretive about himself. He had been born in Russia and migrated during the pogroms to the United States when he was about twelve years old to join his older brother, a journalist in Providence, Rhode Island. For a short time he had been an American schoolboy, atypically old and serious, wearing a formal black suit that must have isolated him from his peers as much as his inquiring mind and his strange foreign accent. He came to New York, still in his teens, to be met by the Depression. It remains a mystery how he managed to move from bread lines, park benches and lonely, hungry sessions in the New York Public Library to found the *Partisan Review* and to become a leading intellectual of the thirties. To some it may appear to be a demonstration of the functioning of our democratic system, but I believe it to be one of those rare glimpses of individual potential, a phenomenon hoped for at all times, in any nation, that relieves and redeems the drab uniformity of universal mediocrity.

Today, whenever I find myself on the porch of a country house, I am transported back to places no longer visited and to people many years gone. A white-shingled corner sheltering a hammock or wicker chair, pillars supporting a separate roof and framing a section of village street, meadow, river, lawn or beach, lazy noon heat, melting salmon pink sunsets or darkness alive with the buzz of cicadas are pieces of one remembrance: summers past. Now from this mosaic I single out Philip and Nathalie Rahv's house in Millbrook, New York, the home, I believe, he loved best. I don't know its precise date but its style belonged to a vanished era. It was generously laid out and decorated on the outside with American gothic fretwork like the House of the Seven Gables. Philip showed us around its echoing rooms and I recognized some of the pieces of modern furniture and abstract paintings from the city apartments. They looked forlorn and lost, scattered over the expanse of bare floors and walls like immigrants stranded on a dock. But, in reverse, these greenhorns were from the New World thrown ashore to make their way on the strange continent of the past. Philip was installing changes, mainly modernizing the kitchen (for him always the heart of any house) and adding bathrooms. Bathrooms represented the acme of luxury, the badge of security, and he counted their number with pride, the left-wing scholar turned squire with the purchase of each new house.

My souvenirs of Millbrook are, in the main, summer ones, as Philip and Nathalie continued to spend their winters in New York City, she to pursue her career, he to run the magazine and to attend those late nights of good talk and gossip that constituted his fuel for living. He would greet his friends avidly, "What's new? Have you heard any gossip?" I always did my best to supply him while he regarded me eagerly like a great beast awaiting the morsel of raw meat I was about to throw him. "I don't believe it!" he would exclaim, running his paw over his head until his black hair fell in disarray. "You must be kidding!" But his own stock of gossip was more copious and hours were spent in hearing about the marital problems of his acquaintances. The substance was usually psychological and analytical rather than vicious. It involved the plots of social or intellectual arrivistes or the sexual eccentricities of writers, many of whom had been launched from the pages of *Partisan Review*, full-grown plants sprung from seeds started in a cold frame within the nurturing atmosphere of a greenhouse. At the dinner hour the gossip would be halted temporarily while Philip performed his kitchen rites with the same didactic sureness he brought to his historical and literary opinions. Saffron rice — its firm jaundiced grain — appeared with every dish. When I taste it now I hear again his soft guttural accents and I see him at the head of his table gobbling his food with the relish of a connoisseur too honest not to appreciate his own creations. He was never able or willing to teach his wives his culinary skills.

On the porch after dinner he would hold forth on politics or on his favorite writers: Tolstoi, Dostoevski, Henry James or Proust and, of course, the eternal triumvirate of Marx, Freud and Trotsky. For contemporary authors, even those he had himself plucked from obscurity, he often showed surprising scorn: "Bah! what's so great about him? Who needs all dose *stetl* fairy stories?" or "Do dey tink dey have invented sex? Dey make me sick!" Saul Bellow was an exception; Philip's endorsement of him grew more emphatic with each book. But in those days his enthusiasm kept pace with his outrage, and for me he opened new worlds of reading. For all his misanthropy, Philip was a born teacher, irrascible, impatient, biased, but just as fire purifies as it destroys, Philip's lectures cauterized the minds of his listeners and provoked in them a kindred spark. Sometimes at Millbrook he would pause to peer over the railing of the porch into the darkness outside and exclaim, "Woodchuck!" in a stentorian voice like that of the old Russian general, Kutuzov at sight of the enemy. "I ought to shoot. Dey are ruining my grass!" And he would make a move toward the gun leaning against the wall of the house. Happily he never used it in my presence — perhaps it was not even loaded but just another prop to reassure himself that he was, indeed, an American landowner who had traveled a long road away from the little foreigner dressed in a black suit in the Providence schoolhouse or the hungry, lonely youth submerged among the dusty stacks of the New York Public Library.

But the time I remember best is a winter afternoon. While summer visits merge with the smells of mown grass and overly rich brown stews, the sounds of cicadas and the sight on the porch at night of the perpetual light of Philip's cigarette like a giant firefly eclipsing nature's fitful competition, the New Year's eve my husband and I spent with the Rahvs in Millbrook remains distinct. It belongs to another time; its characters are costumed in yesterday's finery but it returns every time I think of that house, just as when we

listen to the strains of old songs played on today's stereo the
past reappears to overlay the present.

A few of us had been invited for lunch, although the New
Year's eve celebration would not start before late evening.
Our little group included just my husband and myself,
Mary McCarthy, now married to Bowden Broadwater, a bespectacled, owlish young man who was a librarian in a
snobbish boy's school in New York City, and Nathalie and
Philip. I had never seen the place in winter. The bare
tossing trees and the rough colorless grass stubble without
any flattering cover of snow had a harsh unkempt look.
And the house, starkly revealed, seemed taller than before
and more ramshackle, as though with a gust of winter wind
it might collapse into a pile of timber. Philip met us at the
door in high spirits. He was dressed in the same short-
sleeved sport shirt and slacks he wore in summer, although
the house was cold and drafty, the temperature barely
higher than it was outside. His bearish fat must have kept
him warm. As for the rest of us, we remained bundled in
our coats and jackets. After lunch we huddled close to the
large living room fireplace where a few undersized logs
gave off little licks of flame without warmth and the wind
whistled down the chimney and around the mysterious
dusty corners of the old house. Philip talked on and on,
drinking without cease. A true Russian muzhik — like Ras-
putin — his capacity for liquor was gargantuan, but I
never saw him drunk. With his habitual positiveness he
was denouncing the cold war, but he spoke of his "parlor
pink" colleagues with even greater venom. The contra-
dictory softness and melancholy of his heavy dark eyes in
their dusky pouches moved slowly from person to person,
resting longest, I thought, on the clean-cut handsome face
of Mary McCarthy. As for Bowden Broadwater, Philip took

no more note of him than of a summer insect whose small insignificant life had, somehow, managed to survive into winter. Periodically Philip glanced at his wristwatch, but as we had nowhere to go and nothing to do until the other guests arrived hours later, I could not imagine what he was waiting for. At about four o'clock he announced abruptly, "Now we all put on our eveningh clothes for the party." There was general protest: "so early" — "it's only four o'clock" — "the house is so cold." It was unusual, but formal evening regalia (most importantly for the ladies) had been ordered for this night. Now we were reluctant to expose ourselves to the damp chill of the house. "Upstairs!" Philip commanded and we obeyed. I was the first woman down and found Bowden and Philip already there. Bowden looked slim and stylish in his tuxedo, as though he should have been in the snug rear of a box at the opera rather than in this bare, shabby country living room. "I have just hooked mine up the back," he bragged. "Have you done yours?" he asked smugly. Philip ignored the question. "Mary told me her dress comes from Lanvin in Paris. I have never seen her in a French dress," he said.

Nathalie arrived next. Her clothes made little difference to her appearance. Now her long skirt looked as underplayed as her sweater and skirt. She was a grand lady and could dispense with external trappings.

Mary tarried. Philip seemed as impatient for her arrival as a first-nighter waiting for the curtain to rise. At last she appeared, moving down the uncarpeted stairs, her golden sandals tapping loudly on each bare step like trumpets heralding her entrance. Her dress was red, white and blue in alternating sections. One shoulder was bare, revealing a broad expanse of chest and a strong naked arm. There was no spiky crown on her head but I could see its shadow there and the naked arm holding the torch aloft. Mary McCarthy came slowly down the stairs — the Statue of Liberty in solemn animation, dressed by Lanvin.

Philip watched her with greedy intensity. So this was what he had been waiting for, glancing at his watch so many times in advance, this was why we were shivering in the cold hours before the party. The youthful romantic concealed in Philip's rough exterior had been clamoring to see Mary in her new formal costume. In his big American house he was proud to be host to the renovated version of his early love.

Not long after that night Philip and Nathalie were divorced. It was a shock, although their friends had been aware that the marriage had been shaky for some time. Nathalie, wealthy in her own right and generous, left Philip his beloved Millbrook house. She moved to Boston to continue her work, remaining Philip's friend to the day of his death.

For a while he divided his time between New York and Millbrook. I pictured him solitary on the porch, angrily staring down his old enemy, the woodchuck, while the uncut grass grew higher each day, or in the kitchen surrounded by all his equipment. He could count the number of unused bathrooms, his own always an auxiliary library now more crowded than ever with his reading matter. But it must have been a lonely existence, and Philip was basically a city man. Sadly — it was like another divorce — he sold the house. It had been an American dream that had possessed his imagination and like a dream it slipped away even while he tried to cling to it.

He accepted a professorship at Brandeis University in Waltham. And now in middle age, before it was too late, he went in search of adventure, which for him always meant another woman. He had his teeth capped and, until I grew accustomed to them, they shone out of his swarthy face as brightly as the porcelain fixtures in his bathrooms. He lost weight, bought some new clothes and after many years revisited Europe — the Old World — again. But he soon returned to find his next wife here. After some amorous interludes it was Nathalie who introduced him to Theodora Jay Stillman. She had been a friend of Nathalie's younger sister as Nathalie had been a classmate of Mary McCarthy's at Vassar; so Philip followed a circle from one indigenous American product to the next. Theodora was descended from John Jay, Colonial statesman and jurist.

"Teo iss a lady!" he used to say, and it was true. She looked like an English noblewoman crossed by Gypsy blood in some distant past. She was as tall and massive as Nathalie but she had black hair and flashing black eyes under heavy brows. Her flesh was very white and she seemed to have more of it than most people; it covered her luxuriously like velvet. She had a straight, sharp-tipped nose with long aristocratic nostrils, inherited, perhaps, from her illustrious ancestor. Her mouth was voluptuous and she had a faint mustache. Her lips, usually half open, contradicted the firmness of her jaw and rounded chin. She dressed in bright prints: ruby, purple, emerald. But her hems sagged and the hooks were often missing or the zipper derailed at her ample waist. Philip took pleasure in decorating the white velvet expanse of her décolletage with heavy ornate antique necklaces.

Theo came to him with a house at Martha's Vineyard we had rented years before. One summer I had watched my five-year-old son gathering seashells on the beach in front of it. I remember him stooping in the unindividuated way, the immemorial pose of all children playing at the seaside. Now when I hear the shriek of gulls at once I smell wet salt air, my hair and clothes seem sticky with salt and I can almost feel leftover sand in my shoes. When we returned fifteen years later to visit Theo and Philip the gulls were still swooping over the roof. The same one that had stood sentinel on a tide-washed post in the shallow water of the bay seemed to be there still, motionless, its feathers clear gray and white, like a stuffed bird in a museum, and the sagging hammock, too, strung between two trees on the grass that sloped down to the water. In fact nothing about the house had changed; it had the same bilious sea smell, the peacock fantailed wicker chair, the papery white walls through which one heard a variety of noises: snores, coughs, protesting creaks of beds, and, outside, the everlasting cry of gulls.

"It's all the same! Let me look around!" I exclaimed to Philip as he put my bag down in the guest room.

"This one was ours, do you remember?" I asked my husband as we both looked out the window at the familiar view of the bay where the ferry would still ply its stolid course to the mainland. In the next room we found no disorder of gritty pails, shovels and toy automobiles. The bathroom remained the same, commodious and old-fashioned, like a cottage living room with its chintz curtains and old rocking chair. The well-remembered tub was awkward and high as a Model-T Ford and the collection of family medicines, cosmetics and brushes was still displayed on crude wooden shelves. In another part of the house Theo had built for Philip a more modern bathroom and had made a study out of the attic.

"Oh, it's all the same," we repeated to each other as we clattered from the back stairs to the kitchen. It was all the same, but we were different — ephemeral humans in search of our own pasts, phantoms brushing against the unyielding shell of material things.

As we sat on the porch having cocktails before lunch I observed Philip. He was dressed the same and used the same familiar gestures as when he had been our host in Millbrook. Now Theo was there in place of Nathalie. With a red bandanna covering her head she appeared more Gypsy than English noblewoman. Philip was teaching her to cook without much success. Theo was willing but awkward, and periodically crashes would issue from the kitchen as another piece of crockery was dropped and smashed to bits. Philip remained unperturbed, continuing his discourse on the downfall of the realistic novel or the dangers of a too strong executive branch of the government. He was educating Theo outside the kitchen also. Like an enthusiastic schoolgirl she had shown me her summer reading list; I remember that it included *Jane Eyre* and *Portrait of a Lady*. One of her two daughters, "Little Theo," was there at the time. She was a teenager, extraordinarily tall and thin with long legs in tight jeans. Her beauty was wild and casual, with flowing hair and aquiline features, she looked like a youthful pirate. Philip remained aloof from his stepdaughter, but now and then he threw her a lingering, measuring sidelong glance, in the manner he reserved for all attractive females.

That other holiday with its different cast of characters was far away. There had been picnics on the beach on the surf side where the cliffs frowned over the sand and the waves reared and dashed their foaming heads on the shore. Always there were children in groups and young parents spinning out long days of laziness. A drive to some distant beach, a sail to an island in the morning and barbecues at dusk were the warp and woof of each day. After a picnic on the beach the parents would gather the debris in hampers and pick up the scattered beach toys, then everyone drugged with sun and salt water headed for home.

That evening at the Rahvs' there were guests for dinner, gathered at the candlelit refectory table: Philip Roth on the verge of his great success, *Portnoy's Complaint;* William Styron then working on *The Revolt of Nat Turner,* his wife, Rose, who looked like her name; the playwright Lillian Hellman, bitterly humorous and world-weary, yet romantic, long after, about the staunch Leftists during the vanished McCarthy era; Robert Brustein, drama critic; and a poet whose name I can no longer remember. The conversation was spirited, contentious; still, in the wavering candlelight, I looked across at my husband — was he also searching for a group of children eating peanut butter sandwiches and for our younger selves, gone, but invoked by the well-known house existing unchanged into another age? Where are those years? What were they? — I wanted to cry out to my husband. They were made up of so many things that we took for granted. Let me not take anything for granted anymore. Let the present be meaningful; let it explode so loudly that it drowns out all aching echoes of the past. But this moment too slipped by, and we all rose from the table and moved to the verandah.

"What an extraordinary stole," Rose Styron remarked to Lillian Hellman.

"Dash [Dashiell Hammett] found it for me years ago in Chinatown," she replied, settling the transparent silvery cloud around her shoulders with a depreciatory shrug, as though, exposed to the present scene, it had lost some of its beauty.

We sat facing the water. Philip's voice in the dark led the

rest. He bloomed at night, coming alive in conversation. Sometimes his diatribes, in those soft furry tones, put down current pretentions, hollow trends — more rarely, he praised. Outrage was natural to him, but when he expressed appreciation in speech or essays, though it was always restrained by his strong rationalism, his sincerity and warmth made it seem like a reluctant declaration of love.

"The ferry is late tonight," someone said.

But there it was, appearing broad and dependable, its deck all alight like candles on a birthday cake. We could hear the comforting swish as it went on its way and the mock ferocious blast of its foghorn. In my imagination I could see the ferry pulling up to the dock.

How well I remembered our departure all those years before. My husband, my son and I were leaving the island; the vacation was over. Our bags stood packed at the door and the house, unusually tidy, already looked unlived in. We were all in high spirits, a journey was starting, even though we were only returning home. When we arrived at the dock it was crowded. Although the ferry took off each morning at the same hour, it always gathered an audience. We abandoned the car below and stood on deck looking over the railing. It was a brilliant day and the island was garlanded in sunshine. It had been a good vacation we said to one another, the small annoyances and disappointments forgotten. And we promised ourselves to return next summer. But we never did — and the house was forgotten until many years later with the Rahvs, it reappeared unbidden as a dream.

That night after the dinner guests had gone, we cleaned up and then gossiped, comfortably stretched out on the disheveled sofas. Theo kicked the shoes off her long narrow feet and Philip savored the last tidbits as though he had not already had a surfeit. His insatiable appetite might have kept him up all night but the rest of us were tired. Later, I lay awake for a long time between the cool damp sheets. Through the thin partition I could hear their bed protesting beneath the burden of Theo and Philip's titanic lovemaking, then Philip snoring, Theo's cough; downstairs the clock struck the hours erratically. As day began to brighten the windows, I heard the sea gulls cry and this visit merged with that other one long ago as time collapsed inside the white papery walls of the house and I was ushered into sleep.

After the first visit the house on Martha's Vineyard belonged to the Rahvs alone. No more ghosts from my past came to haunt it. Habit, a relentless killer, had disposed of those frail forms.

Three portraits of Philip Rahv are framed in memory like a triptych. They are over-life-size and they possess an obscure meaning only partially understood. The first, the scene by the well in Bridgewater, Connecticut, is flanked by two set pieces from the Vineyard. Theo, my husband and I used to swim every day in the placid bay near the house. Although we all urged Philip to join us he continued to balk in his lairs: the book-lined study and the kitchen. One afternoon, looking across from the water to the beach, unexpectedly I spotted him, fully dressed, moving ponderously toward us dragging a kitchen chair. We all waved enthusiastically as though witnessing the takeoff of the first blimp. He appeared out of place, sitting stiffly on the uncomfortable wooden chair. Like a Dali painting, his large unassimilated form looked freakish outlined against the smooth stretch of sea, sand and sky. After a few minutes, without any gesture in our direction, he got up and slowly retraced his steps back to the house.

I surprised the third portrait one evening as I was coming downstairs at dinnertime. It was seen through the window on the landing: Philip seated motionless inside a blackberry bower. He was wearing a watermelon pink shirt that emphasized the duskiness of his skin and his black hair. His gross body and his massive head with thick features, shovel-shaped nose, large ears with fleshy lobes a shade paler than his face seemed to crowd the dainty trellis aglow in the setting sun. Framed by the blooming vines, Philip was again the hippopotamus from a faraway land — this time enshrined in natural filigree and the candy colors of a valentine. Again I was arrested by the expression in his eyes. Unaware of being watched they were unguarded, and I saw that they were weighted with a bitter intelligence and an extra load of human sorrow.

The Rahvs' house on Beacon Street was tragedy made material. From the start neither Philip nor Theo were at ease there. Although he was proud of it, its aspect of erstwhile money and gentility was alien to him. I had the feeling that with his solid presence he was attempting to reduce its smugness by subduing it to his differing needs. But it remained strictly Boston Brahmin, despite his garish paintings and, of course, the addition of several new bathrooms. It was as though Philip and some glowering witch-hunting minister out of the American past were locked in combat. Philip was always foe to all pieties. "Bah! Phonies!" he would exclaim, disposing of them with a flap of the hand or a nudge. But the spirit of the house on Beacon Street was persistent. Theo resisted it too. Always loyal and admiring, she was attracted by the Philip of Greenwich Village, the leader of *Partisan Review*, the teacher who supplied her with those reading lists. Now she seemed depressed and bewildered by this return to her own roots from which she was, largely, a refugee.

My memories are of oily dark mahogany wainscoting and banisters, many floors, mostly empty, high ceilings and deep window embrasures. The view across Beacon Street presented similar dwellings high stooped and dingy also. They were now boarding houses, and trash cans lined the sidewalk. Unlike East 95th Street, Beacon Street was on its way down. Philip's house, though privately owned, had undergone a conversion too. In the drawing room, where characters out of a Henry James novel might once have decorously sipped their afternoon tea behind heavy drawn portières, Philip was ensconced with his whiskey and soda. Theo had made muslin curtains for the stately windows, but they were skimpy and looked like dowagers in miniskirts. Here Philip argued with other professors from Brandeis, Harvard or MIT about the cult of illiteracy in contemporary literature and the abuse of freedom from censorship. "Dey tink sex is something clinical — something separate from human feeling," he said. "Dey tink dey are shocking, dey are only boring and ignorant. Such naiveté! Such idiocy!" Theo listened reverently, her mouth with its faint mustache open as if to imbibe his truths. In the kitchen the crockery still crashed, and although the sound was fainter than in the flimsy house on Martha's Vineyard, the kitchen on Beacon Street being far away and the walls thick, Philip, once oblivious, now winced.

With his remove to Boston, his role at *Partisan Review* grew minor. Still editor, he mainly used his power of veto now. It seemed to have overcome his genius for the discovery of talent. His conversation grew more negative too. "It's no good — no good," he would reiterate on almost any subject. But his appetite for gossip remained undiminished. Again and again we heard about the intricate psychological difficulties of the Robert Lowells and stories

about Mary McCarthy's latest marriage to an American diplomat in Paris. My husband brought him all the news he
could gather from New York as though it were a house
present, some cherries or a box of chocolate creams.

The tragedy on Beacon Street reached me one September
evening. I was alone at the time; my husband was in
Europe on a business trip. I believe that it was Bernard
Malamud's voice on the telephone that was harbinger to the
disaster. The night before Theo had gone to sleep with a
lighted cigarette. She was the only one in the big empty
house and when Philip returned the following morning he
found his home gutted and his wife suffocated in her bed.
Of this scene I have two visions: one consists of a heap of
black ashes, the shell of the house a crematorium urn containing the remains of Theo, her white velvet skin reduced
to cinders. In the other, Theo's inert body is draped across
the bed, her head hangs down over the side, her voluptuous mouth wide open, her black eyes shuttered. Dressed
in a virginal white nightgown, she is Desdemona, and
Philip, large and dark, is Othello beholding his wife's
corpse.

One more view of him from that time came to me through
the reports of friends who attended the funeral in Boston.
Philip, always so concealed, was overcome by emotion in
public. He could barely stand up and arrived at the ceremony supported on either side by Theo's daughters. I see
them, two lovely caryatids, dragging his huge form, a griev-
ing gargoyle, down the aisle of the church.

A few days later he telephoned to say he was coming to
New York. I awaited him nervously. All my life I have
been loath to talk of the dead to the bereaved. I remember
that after my mother's death I had allowed my father, in my
company, to remain lonely while I self-protectingly avoided

the subject of my mother. But for Philip's sake I was determined to overcome my cowardice. He arrived looking much as usual, but I was startled to see that he had difficulty negotiating the stairs. He moved like a very old man. His bear hug was warm and so was his soft slurred voice with that thick guttural accent I had grown to love. When we were seated with our drinks, steeling myself, I started to talk of Theo's death. "No! Stop it!" he almost screamed, his heavy kind eyes in their black pouches alive with something close to hatred. "Never mention it to me — never — you understand — you hear me? Never!"

What had I done? What secret spring had been released? Through my long-time affection for Philip I had unwittingly invaded some dark private recess where I had no right to trespass. Aghast, I retreated and the evening resumed its course. Later Philip would come to talk naturally of Theo and her daughters, but in his presence I never dared to mention her name again.

The enigma of his behavior remains and the shadowy antagonisms in the house on Beacon Street are unresolved. Did the spirit of the vanished New England preacher prevail? In wrath, did it punish Philip, the atheistic European outlander? Or was Philip, in some obscure way, the stronger, Theo a sacrifice and the wrecked house a symbol for his burning scorn of traditional bigotry?

Following Theo's death Philip sold the house in Martha's Vineyard that she had left him. Soon after, off season and deserted, it also burned down to the ground. I have not been back to the island so I do not know whether that piece of land is vacant, a missing tooth in the semicircle of white vacation houses fronting the bay, or whether a new building has sprung up on the spot, an intruder on my recollections. They are once more jumbled together in the scrapbook of memory: children's parties, the plodding ferry, beach picnics and Theo and Philip profiled like paper-cutout silhouettes that I have rescued from the flames.

Several summers later Philip visited us at our country home. He brought Peggy Whittaker with him. She was a young divorcée and I knew that he was considering marriage again. He had aged, but his black hair was hardly touched by gray. He lowered himself laboriously down onto the sofa. He seemed contented here; he had always admired our house. Perhaps its rambling form and country furniture, worn with use by five generations of my husband's family, reminded him of some Russian dacha he had glimpsed in his childhood. Or was he merely impressed by the number of our old-fashioned tile bathrooms? "I wanted Peggy to see Purchase," he said, as though my husband and I were the caretakers of some tourist palace: Versailles or Schönbrunn. But his eyes rested on us with affection. I examined Peggy carefully. Philip, now in his sixties, had said when he announced their arrival, "She iss just de right age, tirty-nine!" But Peggy appeared even younger. An instructor at some obscure college in Massachusetts, she looked like a high school student herself — the girl next door. Philip had attached himself to another indigenous American product. She was short and sturdy, built close to the ground. She had a very white smile, cropped gold-tipped hair and tawny skin and eyes. When we were alone Philip asked me several times if I thought her pretty, as though he now doubted even the evidence of his own eyes. He had grown still more negative and was planning to cut all together his connection with *Partisan Review*. "It's no good," he said. "I don't want to be mixed up with those schnorrers anymore." My husband tried to dissuade him but he stood firm. The magazine would fold or it would be supported by suspect funds. Money and literary merit were always antithetical to Philip.

At moments I caught him regarding me with approval tinged by regret. He had been appalled at the happy event of my becoming a grandmother and at the time had commiserated, "Poor Dorotea! It's hard to believe!" Once he had burst out, "You used to be very pretty when you were young!" These were the kinds of remarks his friends and mine resented. "How can you stand him? He's so depressing," they protested. But somehow I never minded his rueful insults, if such they were. I felt them to be proof of his affection for me and of his unflagging honesty. In recent years he had grown increasingly obsessed with thoughts of age and death. But his horror was generous, including those he loved as well as himself. He had told me that at night in bed he stayed awake pondering the ultimate problem of mortality and recoiling in disgust from his own body as though aging were a kind of creeping leprosy.

Peggy arrived for dinner in an apricot mumu. She was weighted down by an elaborate golden parure: a long necklace and dangling earrings that Philip had given her. They would have suited Theo. But Philip watched her with pleasure; he was like someone nipped by frost who finds himself in front of a warm hearth.

Of course, along with a new wife, he acquired another country house, this time in New Hampshire, not far from Boston. Philip and Peggy wintered in Newton, Massachusetts, convenient for the schooling of her young son. "Horribly middle class!" Philip had said about this suburban residence. "It's no good," he added, as though spitting out an unpalatable Howard Johnson's meal. So once more, the city man tried to make himself at home on New

England soil. But something was wrong. On our first and only visit to New Hampshire I was surprised to find the house squatting humbly beside the road. Made of shingles, it was painted barn red and there was a collapsed look about its shape that reminded me of an overgrown chicken coop. In the rear a wire mesh fence enclosed a few dusty zinnias and some weakling vegetables.

Philip greeted us enthusiastically, almost with relief, but he soon lapsed into listlessness. Peggy, by contrast, seemed to be bursting with pent-up energy. When we were by ourselves, she exploded, "I can't get him to leave the house. He just sits all day and night — never writes a word anymore — hardly talks — see what you can do with him."

But we could do nothing. Peggy, my husband and I went swimming in the "lake" nearby. It was shallow, tepid and muddy, but we honestly admired the pristine lines of the white wooden church and the village square. "He doesn't even go to the post office for his mail," Peggy complained as we were driving homeward after our swim.

In the house I was happy to recognize some of the relocated abstract expressionist paintings. They were now like old friends and I welcomed them in this depressed atmosphere. Peggy discussed her Ph.D. thesis; Philip cooked. The saffron rice had not deteriorated, but he ate it with reduced gusto, while he and my husband discussed *Modern Occasions,* the publication Philip had started after his withdrawal from the orphaned *Partisan Review.* To me, the stylized P.R. on the cover had always stood for Philip Rahv and the letters now looked illegitimate. He talked with more animation about forcing them to change their format than about the new magazine. "Where can you get money nowadays?" he asked. But at each suggestion offered by my husband, he grunted, "It's no good — no use," as though the will to failure had now been added to his habitual mistrust of moneymaking methods.

"If he gives this up too, I swear I'll bolt," Peggy muttered. "Look at him!" It was midmorning and Philip was sitting immobile by the kitchen window. He was still wearing his pajamas, bathrobe and scuffs. His bulk was as unmoving as a statue as he stared morosely at the scraggly garden. Of what was he thinking? About his childhood and the dark forests of his native Russia? The excitement of the communist movement in his early days in New York City? The beginnings of *Partisan Review?* Or was he facing down the ugly specters of old age and death that were moving closer with the passing of each day?

On the back porch at night he revived somewhat. Ignoring Peggy's warning about his high blood pressure, he helped himself to another whiskey and settled back to receive the fresh gossip we had collected for him. But my mind wandered as I listened to the cicadas and my eyes followed the tiny flare of Philip's cigarette — also forbidden. Over the porch railing the blackness was total. Where was I? Was this Millbrook or Martha's Vineyard? But Philip did not rouse himself for the woodchuck and I missed the punctual ferry and the breaking waves.

On Sunday morning, our last day, Philip was almost cheerful at the prospect of his luncheon guests, Frances FitzGerald and Alan Lelchuk. He had filled us in the night before. "She iss very beautiful," he had said. "And smart. Her reporting from Vietnam iss good. He iss a professor and iss writing a novel about student revolt at Brandeis. She tinks he iss a real intellectual and he tinks she iss a princess. Her mother is Marietta Tree and when dey visited her he told me Frankie had to show him what knives and forks to use. Probably a lie!" he added. "But it works; each iss something new for de odder. It won't last." But it was obvious that as long as it did Philip would relish his anthropological research.

When Frankie and Alan arrived, due to Philip's prologue it was as though I had met them already. She was tall, blond, clear-eyed; he small, dark and bearded. After he had been introduced to me, he asked, his expression earnest behind his spectacles, "Do you always wear blue? Why?" as though this useless data was of utmost importance to him. He was as inquisitive as a squirrel gathering nuts against the winter season. For Alan, everything was provender for a novel. Frankie, with her candid eyes, was, indeed, lovely. However, it was not until I caught Philip observing her attentively with open admiration that I realized that she reminded me of the young Mary McCarthy. Down the long corridor of years, was Philip viewing his love affair returned in a distant mirror image by the presence of this other young couple?

Alan deferred to Philip. He was both brash and humble, a disciple. But I kept wishing that the master had been the vigorous man I had met some twenty years before on that snowy night at the Kronenbergers' and that he and Alan had been conferring over *Partisan Review*. *Modern Occasions*, too, was a dim mirror image of the original, seen down the same long vista of time. If Philip had been able to read my thoughts I'm sure he would have squashed them saying, "Bah! Who needs to turn de clock back?"

Not surprisingly, Peggy and Philip parted. The marriage had been brief and Philip moved away from the detested middle-class environment of Newton to a bachelor flat in Cambridge. On his rare visits to New York he described it to me. "It has a good view, high up, two bathrooms, its own garage and lots of service — very modern." But it sounded lonely.

He died there, just before Christmas 1973. But because I never saw him in place, his end is not real to me. At times I feel that Philip is still alive and that I may run into him on the street. He will be deep in discourse, vehemently pushing and nudging his companion into the gutter.

Following his death I learned two secrets, as though yielded by the grave since I am certain that Philip would not have divulged them. It was said that in his will he left instructions to give his money to Israel. After a lifetime in the United States, where he had tried to take root through his American wives and his American houses, like an exhausted swimmer who ceases to struggle and, almost with relief, surrenders to the sea, Philip, weary at last, had turned away to sink into the depths of his own culture. And perhaps in dying he accomplished the blending he had sought but failed to achieve by living. His earnings and Theo's inheritance, handed down from her patrician ancestor John Jay, were transfused for the benefit of the Jewish homeland.

The other disclosure reaching me from the grave concerns his name. The man I had known for so many years was not Philip, after all, nor Rahv. That name had been assumed. He was, in fact, Ivan Greenberg.

The Dream

*S*tateroom A was located at the top of the liner. It was the model luxury suite and the most costly. A duplex, the bedroom above was equipped with a gigantic Louis XV bed and the salon boasted a bar as large as an ordinary cabin. French windows replaced the regulation portholes. They were covered by drapes, less unsightly, but no less tenacious than the blackout below. No matter how one pulled and tugged they remained drawn and no daylight or air could penetrate their heavy damask folds. But in Suite A money did procure a very special privilege: a private balcony, no larger than the bathtub protuberances of an average condominium, which could, nevertheless, accommodate two deck chairs. It was strange indeed to see those humble seats that used to casually line the decks of the old steamers transformed on board the QE 2 into objects of extreme rarity. They completely filled the balcony, but a passenger stretched out on their stiff slatted lengths and cozily covered by a nostalgic plaid steamer blanket could see the ocean below and the sky above. For a price, this sight, once the natural right of any voyager, was granted exclusively to the occupants of Stateroom A. But even here there was still no smell of sea. If you were old enough to remember former crossings you might imagine you were detecting that mildly bilious odor by burying your nose in the coarse wool of the steamer blanket. As for the swish of the waves, you were perched too high to hear it, and besides, the deluxe radio concealed behind the gold and white panel in the salon emitted a perpetual barrage of noise that drowned out any other competing sound. Viewed from the snug balcony nature was reduced to a silent picture, no more real than one more image framed inside another television screen.

For the duration of the Young Millionaires' cruise this suite was inhabited by the Johnsons. Chuck Johnson was the youngest member of the club and the wealthiest. Self-made, he had amassed a fortune in traveling medical units used by insurance companies. Despite his success, Chuck remained an unpretentious boy who loved to tinker with mechanical things. He could repair a broken refrigerator or an electric toaster with tender expertise, his hands moving among worldly materials with the ease and respect of a priest handling ritual objects at the altar. He was obsessively concerned with body fitness and in whatever part of the world he might find himself, he always made time for an hour of strenuous jogging. He had a compact, trim, firm physique, neither too tall nor too short, too wide nor too narrow. His features were clean-cut: a chiseled nose and good square jaw. It was often said that the young Johnsons resembled the F. Scott Fitzgeralds.

Nancy Johnson did look like Zelda and she chose to dress in the fashions of the twenties. Sitting at the dressing table in the bedroom of Suite A she contemplated her image in the three-way mirror as she toyed with her ropes of pearls. She was wearing long, droopy chiffon, her ginger hair was modishly frizzy and her narrow green eyes were glazed and worldly wise. Her lower lip protruded in an expression of chronic mild discontent. Yet Nancy's languorous appearance was deceptive — she was an active, militant women's liberationist. And Chuck had had some difficulty in persuading her to join him on this "male chauvinist" cruise, abandoning, for the duration, her female sex instruction group and her classes in primal scream.

As Chuck and Nancy appeared for dinner on the third night out they were both aware of their attractiveness and the admiring glances of the other diners. The vast room (or rather rooms, as the dining halls, like the lounges, were laid out in endless succession) was surprisingly simple. There was no trace of the Ritz, only acres of identical McDonald's restaurants with small crude tables, adorned with the standard ketchup and mustard containers, spread into a horizonless vista.

The maître d' who hastened to greet the Johnsons was inappropriately dressed in formal black swallowtail and white tie. Above his stiff collar he held his raven's head with its crest of black hair proudly. His astonishing eyes covered Nancy from head to toe. For an instant, forgetting her liberation theories, she felt quite fluttery and helpless under his impudent gaze.

Once seated at their table she recovered her poise as she played with her pearls and examined her fellow passengers from under lowered bored eyelids. The Johnsons did experience one rather unsettling moment, when Nancy, upon requesting a knife to spread her caviar, was presented it sharp end first, as though it were a dagger pointed at her heart. Immediately Leopold Litvak, the headwaiter, appeared with profuse apologies for this gaucherie and assurances that it would not reoccur.

As Litvak moved lithely back toward the entrance to greet a new arrival, no one could have guessed the thoughts behind his low broad brow. It was his duty to protect the innocent cruisers from his secret knowledge of the waiters' strike that had occurred at Liverpool on the eve of departure. Rather than cancel the trip, the company had enlisted a group of prisoners, temporarily released from jail, and had hastily schooled them in dining room skills. Litvak was their warden and with his eyes focused upon them the would-be servitors were inhibited from handling *the knives and forks in a fashion more suited to their former life-style.*

Later that night as Chuck and Nancy Johnson were preparing for bed in Stateroom A, she agreed that the cruise might not be so dull after all. Yet she yawned openly as Chuck approached her with those routine gestures that were invariably the prelude to lovemaking. For Chuck, intercourse, like jogging, should be regular — muscles were there to be used. But recently, since Nancy had become such an embattled feminist, he had some-times felt unsure of his virility. His well-trained obedient body had become alarmingly capricious in this respect. Tonight, however, on the deluxe Louis XV bed, his performance was sat-isfactory.

As for Nancy, she frankly admitted to herself that Chuck bored her sexually, but the male role was too insignificant for denial. With the help of her classes she was confidently ar-mored in the conviction that female orgasm was obtainable in a number of ways. She could count on its benefits without plac-ing too much importance on her partner. On the voluptuous bed, covered by Chuck's familiar body, she ignored his vigorous rhythmic thrusts. As she had been taught, she breathed deeply, spreading her ribs wide, and concentrated minutely on her cli-toris. But at the moment of climax, instead of the anticipated response, she was overwhelmed by a mysterious convulsion — during which there appeared, abruptly, the vision of the head-waiter from the dining hall below. He was still impeccable in his black swallowtail and white tie, but his fly was open. In-stead of a phallus, a table knife protruded, extending itself until it reached the proportions of a gleaming sword. At a distance a presence is observing Nancy — and is weaving a dream inside a dream.

THE WORKSHOPS
AND THE RIVER

PHILIP RAHV once described Francis Scott Bradford as a "Fourth of July American." But for a long time to me, clear vision of him was blotted out and he remained a towering silhouette in the strong white north light radiating from the churchlike window of his painter's studio. I observed him with considerable awe, unruffled by understanding. Only since his death has his portrait come together, bit by bit, like the pieces of a jigsaw puzzle.

As often happens, I was nearer to the truth about Brad at our first meeting. I had taken him then for a first citizen of Morristown, New Jersey (a mistake arising from the fact that he was, at that time, working there on a mural for a bank). I noted his impressive height and I had had the feeling that, somehow, his presence was a threat to the flimsy furniture and bric-a-brac in our host's living room. It came as a surprise a few days later to hear a husky unfamiliar voice on the telephone: "I am Thelma Bradford. We met at dinner last week. My husband wants you to sit for a portrait."

In this way I was introduced to the studio on West 67th Street. I have lived in New York City all my life and like most large city dwellers I have carved an enclave out of the vast whole. My village was bordered by the falsely rustic strip of Central Park. Across it the West Side was another country rarely visited. It was chiefly remembered from childhood for a riding stable close to the Bradford's apartment (it has now given way to a broadcasting company). The indoor ring smelled of unventilated earth, fresh horse dung and old leather. New situations creep upon us unaware, stealthily, while we are looking in an opposite direction, so I did not realize that Brad's studio was to become a familiar place annexed to my chartered territory and that it would endure in memory more importantly than the chill airless enclosure of the riding stable mysteriously rescued from the oblivion of the years.

Fifteen West 67th Street is situated in the middle of a block of apartment buildings constructed in the boom period of the 1920s. From outside they are distinguished only by their extralarge studio windows. A few doors away from number fifteen is the Café des Artistes on the ground floor of the Beaux Arts Apartments. That name on the porte-cochère used to conjure up hazy inaccurate pictures of Montmartre. Although I was never inside the Beaux Arts Apartments, it presented a dingy façade in no way different from its neighbors.

On that initial visit the rickety elevator carried me high up above the shabby art nouveau lobby, and as I waited for my buzz to be answered I heard those distinctive footfalls for the first time. They would always be the introductory note to entrance into Brad's studio. For such a large man the steps were surprisingly light, soft, springy and padded like a panther's tread on forest moss. Actually they were made by the rope soles of espadrilles moving over bare wood floors. When the door opened Brad stood before me a complete stranger, quite different from the supposed banker from Morristown, New Jersey, I had met a week earlier. He was wearing a coarse khaki painter's smock. I noticed that his great height was oddly proportioned: comparatively stumpy legs and small feet supporting an elongated torso. His neck was exceedingly long, too, lifting his head high, far from the gravitational pull of his legs. Perhaps I did not discern all this on that first morning as the illumination in the huge room was patchy, alternating pools of brilliant light and sooty darkness, and perhaps the knowledge of his appearance came to me gradually like my familiarity with his place of work.

At the time of our meeting in the 1950s, he was the same age as the century. He looked both young and old. A creature of extremes he seemed to have avoided the compromise of middle age. He had a white tonsure, a broad forehead, the fair rosy skin usually associated with blondness or red hair. His face was rather small and he had a snub nose with sensual nostrils, a long upper lip and a round deeply cleft chin. Despite his age, his face often reminded me of the young Charles Lindbergh. His eyes were deep set and small and of undetermined color, as though their intensity had burned away their original hue leaving only spark and depth. Near them other eyes looked blind. And at times their light was more than human. Prometheus must have had such eyes.

After our greetings he led me to a gilded high-backed velvet chair, a kind of throne on a dais on which I was to pose. I had never sat for a painter before, but any self-consciousness I might have felt evaporated in the lure of that studio: a three-story room with a balcony overhead. Also used as the Bradfords' living room, it was furnished, but sparsely. Sofas and chairs were grouped in front of the cavernous stone fireplace as large as a room itself. Later I learned that, characteristically, the mantel had been built, stone upon stone, by Brad. Above it the pipes of an organ, impressive but mute, rose like the columns of an abandoned temple. The walls were hung with worn brown velvet that absorbed the light like blotting paper. The previous owner had left the Italian furniture, including the golden claw-footed throne on which I was sitting. The studio was a decaying Venetian *palazzo* sinking, not into the sea, but engulfed, instead, by those violent alternates of blinding light and unfathomable shadow.

And what about the work carried forward in that place in those days? It was a contrast to the *palazzo* background. I was to learn that murals are a blending of architecture and painting. Their scale and the necessary properties, scaffold, drawing tables and carpenter's tools belong to building. At this time Brad was making a World War II memorial for a United States cemetery in Cambridge, England. A long strip of paper was tacked to one wall beneath the wrought-iron balcony. The simple, sorrowful forms parading across it in first-draft charcoal were discordant with the filigree coquetry of the perch above, where violinists and cellists should have been playing Baroque chamber music for a gathering of idle Venetian nobles. Instead, Brad, in his workman's smock, labored daily, and in place of perfume the air was filled with the smell of wood shavings, turpentine and paint.

I have always found that the senses, storage houses for the past, are more faithful than the emotions. Not long ago at Avery Fisher Hall I had proof of this. A Mozart symphony was being played and all at once I smelled that amalgam of turpentine, wood shavings and paint — unmistakable and pungent. During the intermission I asked a friend who had been sitting next to me if she too had noticed that odor. "Not at all," she replied. Later I remembered that this Mozart symphony had been a favorite of Brad's and he had played the record over and over in his studio.

The war memorial grew. From my raised throne, Brad became a familiar figure. He stood in front of his easel, his paintbrush in his right hand, another brush sometimes clenched between his teeth and in his left hand the streaked palette that looked like the shield of Achilles. He was having difficulties and would not permit me to see behind the impassive canvas back. In the end, dissatisfied, he destroyed the large oil painting. I have been left with a quick preliminary water-color sketch. I do not recognize myself in this impression: I am dressed in black, wasp-waisted, and resemble a drooping ebony hothouse lily. Dating from the same time I also own a life-size charcoal drawing of my head — different but equally strange to me. I'm wearing a prim poke bonnet beneath which my eyes look out, clear and stern, like a Salvation Army miss. Both portraits hang on our guest-room walls and I rarely look at them. If I do, they no longer have any connection with their creator, nor do they bring back that lofty room that now seems part of a dwindling dream reluctant to be coaxed into the waking world.

The war memorial remains in memory: one head, in particular, attracted me. Though androgynous, it was strongly sexual — dark and mysteriously seductive, with a trumpet nose, flaring nostrils and wild eyes. I took it to be the angel of death and the fallen bodies of the young soldiers seemed to be pulled from their prone positions on the ground by an invisible current — upward — to where it soared, a wild wind drawing them like a magnet, irresistibly, with evil force.

One day when I arrived early for my sitting I found the model for this angel of death seated on my golden claw-footed throne. I recognized the winged eyes and the tumbled black hair. She was a Frenchwoman, young and chic, rendered by Brad's imagination into that avenging spirit. As though she were my rival I felt a stab of jealousy. Her image was destined to be for the public in the Cambridge memorial while Brad's unsuccessful efforts with me, resulting in those flimsy drawings, were eventually to find their humble way to our spare bedroom.

Easel painting was his recreation. "I am a Sunday painter," he often said. But as I observed him this occupation did not appear to bring him peace, and he seemed far more confident perched precariously on a ladder, looking like a house painter confronting the magnitude of a mural.

The war memorial, completed, was shipped to England and Brad and Thelma followed for its installation there. During the preceding months my husband and I had grown to be friends of the Bradfords'. Through the years I learned something of the story of his life. Although Thelma always romanticized everything connected with her husband, her garrulousness and his rare utterances about himself combined to give me a glimpse of his background and to put together his past up to the time we met.

Francis Scott Bradford was born in Appleton, Wisconsin, in full summer during the last year of the nineteenth century. I picture his birthplace: the upper-middle-class residential street lined with trim solid houses shaded by old elms. I see a boyhood in which nature was always nearby: lakes, ponds, swimming holes, outlying fields and farms. And I see the young Brad, ancestor to the man I knew, attentive to this multifaceted world of rotating seasons: the appearance and disappearance of wildflowers, tall grasses, the hiding places of birds, frogs, insects, fish and deer. He was at home on the Spartan prairies and in the cathedrallike mysteries of deep forests. But I see him turning away in disgust from the cluttered parlors, plush and horsehair upholstery, scrupulously scrubbed floors and smug lace curtains. Early in life he rebelled against the Protestant religion belonging to his forebears and observed by his own family in dutiful conformity. He had deserted the Bradford pew in the ugly fieldstone church whose interior was obscure and stuffy, parsimoniously unadorned. And he had turned a deaf ear to the droning perfunctory sermons of the local minister. Eventually, he had rebaptized himself an atheist, to the horror of his mother and his twin sisters. Spinsters, I see them like nuns manqué — always together, conserving the strictness of their ancestral home. His forebears had arrived in America on the *Mayflower*, eventually pioneering westward to Wisconsin where they had settled. After his parents' death Brad had no desire to return there to renew himself in his native land, in his roots.

Brad's father had been a judge, and he spoke of him with loving respect. I imagined him as having the sterling qualities of an Abraham Lincoln. An old photograph confirmed this resemblance: bony hawklike face and intelligent, kind, weary eyes. He and Brad had only their great height in common and Brad was always envious of his father's aquiline profile. He once told me that when he was a child his mother used to place a clothespin on his nose to pinch it into proper narrowness.

When the United States was drawn into World War I, Brad left Appleton and joined the army. At eighteen he was leading a battalion of men twice his age (related by Thelma). The only story of the fighting he told me himself concerned his encounter with a dying German soldier. "He had flaxen hair and pale blue eyes — and he was so young," he said, forgetting that his own age had been the same. He had asked Brad for a drink of water in a matter-of-fact voice and then quietly, without any drama, he had died in Brad's arms. For many years Brad dreamed about this meeting. But he continued the fight, undiminished, until a bullet in his head arrested him and he was invalided out of the army, receiving a silver plate in his skull and numerous decorations.

It was while he was recuperating in a rehabilitation center in Indianapolis that he had his first experience in painting. For therapy he was sent to a nearby art school where he discovered his own virtuosity, and his enthusiasm for art untapped riches. "Imagine," he used to say. "We never saw a painting in Appleton, not even a reproduction. We had plenty of books but illustrations were considered frivolous."

After the war it was taken for granted that he would return home, finish college and take up law like his father. He agreed, but his taste of art school caused him to beg his father for one year in New York City — just that time to indulge in painting. His father agreed and even offered him financial aid, small, but as much as he could spare. His mother and sisters were convinced that he had started down the road to perdition. "My father visited me once in New York City," Brad told me. "He sat in silence close to me while I was painting. We were totally apart, but I felt he was trying to understand me and what I was doing. We were separated by more than miles — and yet the bond between us was stronger than ever."

I see the youthful Brad at this period, a loner in the city, not part of any Greenwich Village group, oddly formal and correct in his poverty. "I studied at the Art Students'

League all day and in the evening I usually went to the Chinese laundry to wash my only good shirt." This was said without self-pity. It was just a statement of fact. And, anyway, he was returning to Wisconsin at the end of the year.

But luck, that prime mover, intervened. Brad, barely started on an uncertain career, won the Prix de Rome. He whose whole experience of Europe had been the battlefields of France was to have a year, paid for this time, at the American Academy in Rome. It was not to be refused.

The Academy, a luxurious villa, is situated on the Janiculum Hill in the midst of a tropical garden. It combines the seductiveness of a Garden of Eden with monastic dedication to the arts. In those days, protective rule removed the students from the beckoning fascination of the old, knowing, wicked, beautiful city just below the confines of their rosy walled ivy-covered jail.

But more than the prize, more than the Indianapolis rehabilitation classes, it was an almost indescribable event (lasting perhaps one minute) that once and for all changed the course of Brad's life. He often attempted to describe it to me but it was not until I saw Rome myself that I began to understand. One day while he was standing near the statue of Garibaldi looking at the view from the top of the Janiculum, the city clustered about the giant beehive dome of Saint Peter's beneath a great sweep of sky where the scudding clouds appeared more living than the panorama of the Eternal City, time and space suddenly merged for Brad. He felt himself melting into immensities, as though his arms were being stretched infinitely wide in an inclusive embrace of all he surveyed — and beyond. He lost himself in a kind of swoon — for only an instant — but when he recovered, although still upright, everything was different.

It was as though he had shaken his fetters. He knew that he would never return to Appleton and to the law — even his father no longer mattered. He was determined to become a painter. He would follow that life whatever it might bring.

In the 1920s murals were popular and Brad, always attracted by monumentality, chose to become a muralist. When I browsed through the old scrapbooks in his studio it was hard for me to believe that he had made those overly sweet Puvis de Chavannes–like compositions or the allegorical neoclassical representations of Liberty or Justice blindfolded with her scales. They had proliferated in courthouses, banks, city halls, schools and post offices across the country.

One afternoon I accompanied Brad to an exhibition at the National Academy of Design: period pieces in an old-fashioned cluttered gallery. And I remember, on leaving, that Brad had looked wistfully across the street to where the Guggenheim Museum presided over Fifth Avenue like a giant white snail. "Everything is a relief from something else," he had said, adding with bitterness, "did you know that I'm probably the foremost muralist in the United States? But there are only about five of us left and we are all dinosaurs."

After his first year at the American Academy in Rome Brad and his work were in demand. He was no longer the loner who had washed his shirt at the Chinese laundry in the hope of a stray invitation. Now he attended parties at houses in New York City, Long Island and Connecticut, often decorated by his murals. He was always attracted by rich fabrics, fine wood, costly marble and beautiful well-dressed women. But the Puritan buried deep inside him regarded the latter with suspicion and a certain fear. He could be tempted by these females but they remained for him like the glittering snake in the Garden of Eden, and when he came to marry he did not pick a bride from the ranks of "those pampered industrialists' daughters." Instead, he chose Thelma. Her background was so obscure and she was so unspoiled that chameleonlike she could change to suit his every need. Resourceful and practical, she adapted to the rich years as well as to the lean. The Bradfords were childless and she was free to occupy herself solely with her husband and Toby, their large black poodle.

They returned from England with photographs of the Cambridge War Memorial. We looked them over one rainy winter afternoon sitting in front of the cavernous stone fireplace, ablaze now with a feudal flame that turned the rest of the studio into a palace of shadows. I observed Thelma, small, pigeon-plump with chestnut curls, white skin and green eyes. She might have resembled a child bride grown middle-aged except for the shrewd expression in her eyes and the determination of her firm chin. Her hands were never idle: sewing, shelling peas or knitting while she listened to Brad with the rapt attention of a devoted but somewhat muddled pupil. His topics were numerous and he was didactic and vehement. A man of passions as contrasted as the light and dark inside his studio — hate the British, love the Italians, no to the fluid perfection of Greek nudes, yes to the angularity of Egyptian figures, no to the stone imitation lace of Gothic spires, yes to the solid nobility of the Romanesque, to the Etruscans, the Byzantines and the gorgeous entanglements of the Renaissance fountains of Rome. Yes to all dedicated craftsmen, no to pretentious artists. The violence of his negative reactions would cause a flush that suffused his forehead and cheeks, even his pugnose and cleft chin with an angry red. While lecturing he would pace up and down the bare floor in his blue espadrilles, still light-footed and pantherlike, and to those who did not know him well he might have appeared fierce. But when he quietly pored over a book of Byzantine mosaics, Empress Theodora in her stiff golden and jewel tone robes or two doves eternally drinking from a round stone basin, he would purr with satisfaction, the fierce panther gentled, for the moment, into a cat before a bowl of cream. In music, Brad preferred the celestial clarity of Haydn, Bach, Mozart and Vivaldi to the storms of Beethoven and Brahms. Yet when he listened to the dark contralto voice of Kathleen Ferrier singing lieder, I would catch a fugitive unguarded tenderness in his eyes. In reading he was drawn to the classical heroics of Homer and Virgil and to the philosophers of the Enlightenment. He considered the beloved *War and Peace* a soap opera.

While Thelma and I drank five o'clock tea, Brad enjoyed refueling with his first bourbon of the evening. We passed the viewer with its slides of the Cambridge War Memorial from hand to hand. I saw a sea of undifferentiated small white crosses stretching away from the mausoleum that housed the mural. On the slides it looked crowded and unrecognizable. And I knew that now that his work on the mural was over any reminder of the 1939–1945 war filled Brad with frustrated rage. He had again offered himself for combat, but this time, because of his wound and his age he had been rejected. Due to his record in World War I he was commissioned with a high rank and relegated to a desk job in Maryland. Caged in his office, tripped by the strings of bureaucracy, I was sure his face must have been an even deeper red than when he was expounding his no categories in the studio. His heart literally burst, and he suffered a severe coronary attack from which he almost died. It left him with only a sliver of a functioning heart, an even deeper wound than the one he had sustained in the first war. So when I met him he was a sick man living on borrowed time. But he never appeared that way; to me his damaged heart was another field of battle and Brad the invincible general, but he believed his wars were now contained between the covers of books about Napoleon's campaigns that he read for relaxation when his day's work was done.

When the day was over Thelma and Brad used to enjoy entertaining. Their gatherings were large and festive. At these times Thelma took over; she was the general who sought and captured the architects who might supply Brad with the employment he needed. She created the dishes in the kitchen with the sureness of a munitions expert and interpreted to her guests Brad's principles on every subject, in her simplified version. They sounded abrasive delivered in that husky, breathless voice of hers. Today, in the era of women's liberation, I sometimes think of Thelma reigning at night in her Italianate palace, dressed in full evening regalia, looking like a domesticated Scarlett O'Hara. Tiny and bristling with energy, her plump body was pulled in tightly by the waist-cincher in vogue in the fifties. It gave her the contours of a pincushion in the shape of an hourglass.

More aloof, Brad would circulate among his guests. In his impeccable tuxedo he looked distinguished, his black bow tie setting off his surprisingly youthful cleft chin. He was again that "first citizen" of our original meeting, with the difference that now the painter in his rough khaki smock, holding his streaked Achilles shield palette, followed the formal host like a persistent shadow.

The studio was transformed for these occasions. The

working equipment was somehow pushed out of sight. The northern light in the cathedral window gave way to an elegant night view of New York City skyscrapers. And there was no contrast of blinding light and shadow, only an even glow in which the Italian furniture looked less shabby. Its sparseness had been supplemented by the caterer's chairs and even the golden claw-footed throne had been pressed into service as an armchair. Once the Bradfords hired a string orchestra to play from the balcony overhead. But for me the imagined musicians and nobles in the empty studio were more authentic. The faint smell of paint, turpentine and wood shavings lingered reminiscently in the air.

The guests were varied, but one was always aware of the phalanx of architects: I can recall Wallace Harrison, looking like a prosperous capitalist with a hint of the out-of-doors Westerner about him, an urban ex-cowboy. Max Abramovitz, his partner, small, dark, clever, resembled a City College graduate student who had made a connection with the thriving dude ranch of Wallace Harrison. At that time they were started on the Lincoln Center project. Also present was Percival Goodman, the brother of the radical "hippie" precursor Paul Goodman. Percival Goodman seemed to be clinging by a toehold to his brother's brave new world and he looked wilder and more left-wing than his youth-arousing sibling. And there was also old Ralph Walker, once famous. But what had he done lately? Was he, perhaps, a fellow dinosaur?

I am able to recall with a special clarity a series of drawings for some tympana to go in the national Catholic cathedral in Washington. The inappropriateness of an atheistic ex-Protestant portraying conventional ecclesiastical subjects for a Catholic church never occurred to me. The rendering was rugged. The central figure of Christ appeared on a crude seat of which he seemed to be a part; half man, half throne, he was the very image of power. Where was the submissive martyr, that saintly face as accustomed as a family portrait to most Catholics? The flanking panels have grown hazy now, but I do recall the Good Samaritans and Father Damien landing on the Island of the Lepers. The total effect was stark and severe but suffused by an underlying, understated reverence, more puritanical than papal. These drawings had succeeded the War Memorial. The angel of death, almost sentimental by comparison, had disappeared. One evening I discovered Denise, the Frenchwoman, model for that Medusa head, among the guests at a party. But without the reinforcement of Brad's vision, she appeared quite ordinary, a Parisian *vendeuse* or a pretty dispenser of *patisseries.* My former jealousy had vanished also.

The cathedral mosaic was made in Florence and Brad returned to his studio filled with memories of Italy as warming to his mind as were his nightly bourbons to his body. For him Italy was always an intoxicant: the ancient land bearing the ruins of classical times, aqueducts, walls, serene tombs guarded by pointed dark cypress trees and formal Renaissance gardens that overcame the severity of nature. But the cities were best — Rome, of course, first — a coffer of perduring stones. And there were the accounts of his helpers, expert artisans sprung from generations of workers in mosaic: Pietro, Mario, Luca. Brad respected their expertise and I know that he found comfort in their company and was never irrascible or scornful as he was when obliged to court the New York City architects. But commissions were necessary. It was a minor death to be without work. Yet when the desired transaction was achieved he was often let down and disillusioned. "What do they want?" he would thunder. "A postage stamp pasted on a wall of a completed building? I should be called in for the planning or not at all." But he accepted whatever was offered. Having been without work for some months, he had agreed to paint a mural for a public school in the Bronx. On a dreary winter's day he drove Thelma and me to the site. After Italy, the ugliness along the way must have been an especial affront: the hot dog stands, the billboards, the housing developments. Where a chain restaurant, the White Castle, a hideous plaster crenelated tower, came into view we turned off and soon came to the newly finished raw school building planted in a swamp. Inside it was cold and damp. Brad's mural was in the low-ceilinged vestibule; his work looked apologetic and sallow painted in bilious greens. Thelma and I shivered inside our coats and my heart was heavy. I glanced at her and wondered whether she was sharing my feelings. Brad changed into his smock and mounted the scaffold. From his lofty perch he was a commanding figure, the master builder at work.

Easel painting could rasp his nerves. He was always groping for the unreachable and his successes were often inadvertent. Once I found a roll of discarded wrapping paper on the floor of the studio. Opened, it revealed Hebe, the cupbearer of Greek mythology. The painting was done with free abstract strokes. A winged drapery was flung across one shoulder, the long stiff black hair like a coif was Egyptian, the green pitcher she carried, an Etruscan bronze, but the nude herself was boldly original. Dusky reddish brown, in profile she revealed one full, firm breast, a flaring hip and round buttocks. He had arrested her in sinuous motion. Topping a long slender reedlike throat the face was disproportionately small; featureless, it seemed to be floating triumphantly disengaged from the extravagantly female torso.

"I like this," I said.

"Oh, it's nothing," he replied. "I was only trying out poster paints for a panel I am doing for a party at the Century Club."

"I want it."

It hangs in our home today. When Brad saw it ironed out, framed and in place he looked surprised. "It's not bad," he admitted. "I wish I knew how I did it."

His strivings were not confined to murals and easel paintings. Inside the Venetian studio he dreamed of an ideal college — the Etruscan University — where workshop skills were to be taught along with mathematical and philosophical abstractions. It is, perhaps, fortunate that this project never saw the light of realization. He also planned a Utopian city of the future. In a reduced version this creation nearly came to be. My husband introduced it to a foundation concerned with urban renewal. I sat in on a meeting when Brad, aflame with missionary zeal, expounded his theories and exhibited his meticulous miniature model: a plaza surrounded by low buildings equipped to house hundreds of people. The development would be self-sufficient with its own shops and areas for entertainment — a hamlet oasis within the big city desert. It would be just as functional and economical as the desolate highrise condominiums springing up on all sides and it would restore to the poor the sociable stoop life from which they were being routed. In the center of the plaza Brad, of course, had made a fountain that would spurt a generous jet of water. Pale, earnest and sober the committee regarded Brad as a wild artist, a failed Leonardo da Vinci, who would be wiser to stay with his paints and canvas and leave city planning to specialists who knew better. But they listened to him politely and examined the model. In the end the plan was filed, but not before thousands were spent on research. Then, happy with their safe conservation of reports inside steel cabinets, the board members abandoned the project. The plaza was never built. It had joined the Etruscan University in the realm of dreams.

Brad was always irresistibly drawn to competitions. He entered them gaily, filled with hope and zest, but a little embarrassed, as though he were sporting a tie and a suit too youthful for his present age and position. Perhaps the contests were an echo of that original that had won him the Prix de Rome long ago. I remember the struggle in the studio to achieve a memorial for Franklin D. Roosevelt — a man Brad did not particularly admire, perhaps one of the reasons for his difficulties. But the winner would have his work enshrined in Washington, companioned by the George Washington and Thomas Jefferson monuments, and Brad venerated the Founding Fathers of the Republic. But the work, a modernistic Stonehenge, progressed haltingly. Brad was restless and angry, as though locked in combat with a wily enemy.

One afternoon Thelma and I, returning from a shopping expedition, found him absorbed, bent over his worktable. Even the angle of his elongated back looked belligerent. At our arrival he stopped with relief. After fortifying himself with two bourbons in preparation for an appointment with one of those "obtuse obdurate architects," he changed from his smock into a somewhat shabby tweed coat and he and I left the studio together. We were both silent, in deference to the pent-up storm brewing inside him. We walked eastward toward Central Park. It must have been fall or early spring because, although it was late afternoon, the sky was still light and clear. At the corner the Café des Artistes was being renovated and a can of paint had been overlooked on the sidewalk in front of it. Brad, darkly abstracted, not looking where he was going, kicked it over. The oily liquid spread across the asphalt, like a grass green hemorrhage. He stopped dead in his tracks, watching the flood spill out of the overturned pail. I was struck by the expression on his face: awe and recognition, as before a miracle.

"Do you see it?" he asked. "I have it at last. This is it. This is what it is all about!"

At first I thought he must be talking about the solution to the problem of the Roosevelt memorial left unsatisfactorily incomplete up in the studio. But the expression in his eyes negated that idea. He was obviously lost to past moments as well as to the present. Time was stopped. Like a man who has just broken out of the bars of a prison cell, he looked dazed but free. Although I could only see a can of green paint spilled over grimy pavement, I sensed, somehow, what he was experiencing and understood that it was related to that moment in his youth when, standing at the top of the Janiculum Hill in Rome, the course of his life had suddenly been altered.

The mystical intrusion was over as abruptly as it had begun. Reaching Central Park West we bade each other an ordinary goodby and continued our ways in differing directions. Neither of us referred again to what we each had seen.

Fall and spring weekends and summers the Bradfords spent at their home in Cornwall Bridge, Connecticut. One afternoon (in what turned out to be the last year of his life), I ran into Brad on Fifth Avenue in front of the Frick Museum. It was a cold, windy, invigorating day, but it must have been April because the magnolia tree in front of the gallery was in full bloom. The fleshy pink blossoms tossing before the Georgian stone mansion looked opulent and joyous. A scene for Brad to relish, but he appeared sad and tired. And the nitroglycerin pills he usually popped into his mouth as casually as though they were gumdrops now seemed medicinal though unavailing. I felt shaken by the proximity of his illness. It was the middle of the week, but he said, "We're going to Cornwall. It's stifling cooped up in the studio — I'm famished for the country."

I realized that his lofty workshop and the city, festively bedecked anew for spring, were not the causes for his suffocation. It was taking place within his own rib cage: he was slowly being choked by the overtaxed fragment of his heart.

The Bradfords had bought their house in Connecticut many years earlier when they were first married. Riversedge was an eighteenth-century farm perched on a small rise next to the broad Housatonic River that ran beneath the foothills of the Berkshires. In some rooms the river could be heard, at times softly like a cradle song, at times in a rushing roar. In storms the Housatonic would flood the land and threaten to swallow the white house with its neat garden that had the temerity to rest so close to the river's imperious course. It was then that I heard stories of how Brad took over. He fought the flood, secured the house and rescued his neighbors, working day and night without stopping. Legends of battle still clung to him. He would always accept war as a violent fact of nature, like electrical storms and the angry unleashing of his familiar river.

Inside the studio barn across the road the noise of the river was shut out, replaced by the more subtle, less insistent sound of the brook. It spoke of the woods it ran through, of leafy enclosures, shade and mysterious shafts of light, waterfalls and whirlpools, the smell of humid fungus and dry pine needles, the intricate designs of fern lace and deep tangled roots.

Turning off the main route into the back road that led to Riversedge one was met by an onrush of freshness rising from the river as it flowed and curled over the smoothly worn rocks that lay in its bed. And always the clarity of the air and the water raised one's spirits — giving promise — of what? Small, but brilliantly white in the midst of summer greenery, the barn at first sight looked challenging, like the panoply of a general's encampment on the eve of some historic battle, and the clamor of the river became the sound of distant trumpets.

Brad would be waiting for us on the lawn in back of the house. Toby, the large black poodle, would bound around us and Thelma would greet us with effusive hospitality. Brad moved more slowly behind her with the good coordination and dignity of those who are able to forget themselves. Although his towering frame seemed too large for this setting he invested it with special significance. The conventional black-shuttered house, the stone urns (holding begonias and petunias) he had brought back from Italy, a colony of bird-houses he had built himself — all these simple things had become valuable because he had worked on them, because he loved them.

In the afternoon we would wander over to the barn. It was a rustic room filled with workbenches, sawhorses and tools, and smelling of wood shavings, paint and turpentine. Here, as in the city, Brad would bring out his work to show us. The stacked canvases would be separated and placed, one by one, on the easel. Or we would lean over the blueprints on his drawing board while he explained a projected mural or rummaged through a pile of glass or marble mosaic, holding out a piece for us to admire like a child with a prized seashell. I remember a proposition for a wildlife museum, a *trompe-l'oeil* painting in brilliant color, in imitation of mosaic. Birds and small animals were enclosed inside irregular squares partitioned by thick black lines. The Byzantine influence was there, but the animals derived from his Midwestern boyhood. The simplicity of this mural was far removed from the Puvis de Chavannes allegories and the blindfolded Justice in the scrapbooks. Age and experience were needed for a lighthearted work like this. Brad lost the competition to a contestant who depicted outdoor life in lurid scenes, like a still version of a Western film.

Sometimes a painting on an easel would reach out to me and everything else would fall away. There was a strange figure of a little man — a child, dwarf or sprite? He was holding a flute and was seated in a field of tiger lilies beneath a primitive moon. He and the land and the night sky appeared to be attentive to an invisible power — listening, in unison, to the hushed voice of silence. I felt that I was standing close to the materialization of that invisible goal Brad was always battling to reach. And I looked at him for confirmation of this moment. As always, nothing escaped his eagle's glance and he was grateful for my response. But I saw that he would not rest, that he could not stop, even momentarily. So much was under way here that I often felt the old barn must rock and split its sides from the tumult generated within and the hot afternoon sun without, beating down on its gabled roof.

Later we would have drinks on the lawn, and the evening train, a necklace of light, would rattle past at the base of the mountain across the river. I enjoyed the cooling air, our voices against the sound of the river and the sight of Brad's hand, a white patch in the dusk, resting gently on the black woolly back of Toby.

During that last summer I and all his friends realized that

he must die soon. That is, we knew it when we were away from him. In his presence, his plunging eyes defied such knowledge. He was aware of his condition and did not evade the truth, but he rejected sympathy and useless regrets with all the fierce will of his nature. His way of living continued the same. He still climbed the scaffold to work on a mural, the canvases still multiplied in the barn and like the good craftsman he was, he still delighted in forging a fender for the fireplace or building a fountain for the garden. Life continued the same, but was more precious. Each ordinary hour at Riversedge became an extraordinary gift: from the early morning wisps of vapor on the mountaintop to the light of the moon that turned the river to phosphorous. And we who were with him that summer shared in this enhancement. Near him we were supported by the final push of prodigal vitality that sometimes emanates from those in constant danger. We followed where he led.

There was no change either in Brad's appearance. He still looked rugged and ruddy. In fact, he seemed to have taken on even greater stature as he turned his face squarely and unflinchingly toward his last and most worthy adversary. But very often during the day he would hastily swallow those pills that made it possible for him to go on working. His blunt capable fingers fumbling in the tiny pillbox were strangely incongruous, like those of a carpenter learning to take snuff. His doctor friend used to shake his head over him. "There are some things that medicine can't explain," that wise man said. Medicine could do nothing now but stand on the sidelines and watch the miraculous battling of the human spirit.

The last time I visited Riversedge I went alone. When the local Toonerville Trolley train stopped at the Cornwall Bridge station Brad was waiting on the platform. He looked tall and unsteady; there seemed to be more distance than ever between his head and his legs. A scarlet kerchief was knotted around his long throat. Like a signalman's flag, it meant danger to me.

It was a late summer's day, just past Brad's sixty-third birthday on August 17. He had shown me one of those flippant cards sent him on that occasion by his sister, Josephine. He seemed pleased by it — perhaps because in spite of so many obstacles he had, after all, achieved sixty-three years. Or, maybe, he enjoyed memories of his youth in Appleton of which those sisters were a part, and perhaps their strictness and bigotry had paled because he was ready to accept them now as links in a weakened but still existing family chain.

In the hot afternoon he and I sat on the lawn of Riversedge. He was watching the river and I was looking at him, surreptitiously trying to memorize his profile, the lift of his chin. He sat motionless, absorbed by the moving water, which changed as it parted and foamed, rippled and churned around the boulders. Yet it was always the same, too, one flowing path of endless continuity. Although he sat on the shore I sensed he felt assimilated into its mighty flux. For once a kind of peace issued from him. He was looking directly at the enemy, but this time there was victory in acceptance. I was excluded, he had deserted me. But my sadness was shot through with a current of vicarious triumph. Life and death were right here — so present that they were almost palpable, like the feel of the rough sun-warmed stones of the wall or the cold slippery surface of the rocks in the water below. When Brad turned, at last, his eyes were an impenetrable slate color. They seemed to be made of the very substance of the river.

*

At seven o'clock in the morning the telephone rang. I heard Thelma Bradford's husky voice saying, "Brad is dead." The news was a physical blow, as though the ground had opened up in an earthquake or an avalanche had descended on the house.

Autumn had begun and the country was shrouded in thick fog as my husband and I traveled the familiar way. When we turned in by the river, it was almost hidden in the sickly mist, and the usually bright autumn foliage looked limp and yellow; no fresh exhalation rose from the water. We passed the studio; it already looked dim and closed down. As usual, Toby bounded out to meet us, but I could not bear to look at him. He reminded me, somehow, of the riderless horse that follows a military funeral cortege.

In the house Thelma was surrounded by a group of bustling women I had never seen before. They were trying to be helpful but I was hostile to their presence, as though they were barbarian invaders.

We sat on the sofa with Thelma while she repeated again and again how he had died the way he wanted to — in his home, surrounded by the things he loved. He went suddenly, with his eyes wide open. There had been none of the clinical paraphernalia of sickness. He had not been sick; his heart had simply cracked and stopped and he had fallen like a tree struck by lightning. Then why were these strange women here, brimming with funeral ritual?

Nothing in the house had changed and yet it looked withered and drab. I averted my eyes from his paintings staring boldly from every wall. Someday I would be grateful for them, I would be able to look at them again and see them apart from him. But now I felt an animosity to all inanimate objects that persisted, that would obdurately outlast him for all the years to come.

Thelma was answering the telephone, speaking to the undertaker, the minister, thanking departing neighbors, greeting arriving ones. Everything had a ghastly irrelevance. I sat stiffly on the sofa, waiting for the moment of release and hoping that my mute presence was in some way companion to her feverish desperation.

When my husband and I finally drove away, I had the feeling I would never see Riversedge again. After so many years it would be gone. But memory can be irrepressible and, for a long time, Brad's place returned to haunt me whenever I saw a river hastening to its unknown destination or when I heard the noisy shudder of a train at dusk.

Now many years later the pieces of the puzzle are drawing together. The background was completed long ago: the Venetian palace, the Revolutionary farmhouse, the white barn. But the jagged edges of the man did not fit. Brad, the self-made atheist, was a mystic in spite of himself. Could it be possible that if chance had caused him to live in the eighteenth century instead of the twentieth the artist, whose search always seemed too heavy a burden for his paint and canvas to bear, might, instead, have been a pioneering preacher? The parts are meshing at last. Brad appears alone, separate from his studios. The picture emerges in clear outline and strong color revealing to me, too, a genuine Fourth of July American.

There is an epilogue to Riversedge. True, I never saw the house again; it burned to the ground taking all Brad's paintings with it the winter following his death. But after Thelma married Ralph Ingersoll, newspaper publisher, editor and writer, they built another home on the same site.

Not long ago my husband and I were asked to a party at the Ingersolls'. It was my first return to Riversedge. The drive was so habitual that years later it was hard for me to believe that Brad would not greet us on his driveway and that Toby would not be dashing around the car in joyous hospitable circles. When I arrived I realized that I had not seen the barn. Perhaps the general's panoply had been removed to another encampment. Or, the charged air inside the studio having been dissipated, the bright white wood walls might have collapsed and been reabsorbed into the dark forest from which they had issued. Later I found out that the barn was still standing and was now used as a guest cottage. How had I overlooked it? Thelma met us, somewhat older, her small plump body more set, her chestnut curls untinged by gray, her white skin drier, more papery. She was as amiable as ever and as garrulous. Behind her followed, slowly, not Brad but Ralph Ingersoll. He was almost as tall as his predecessor but swarthy instead of fair, impressive in his own fashion, old now, in his seventies (it was difficult to believe that Brad would have been the same age). Thelma, always the good wife, was still voluble about her husband's occupations, but now pigments, marble and architecture had been replaced by journalism.

There was a large crowd standing outside on the lawn. It was a warm late summer night. Lanterns had been strung up on the trees and I noticed that the colony of birdhouses had vanished. In place of the bare trestle picnic bench, banquet tables were covered with pale cloths, blanched ghostlike in the moonlight. They looked like open caskets waiting to receive their dead.

The party almost drowned out the sound of the Housatonic, but I could just distinguish it running like a thread of memory through the general noise. Standing on the familiar embankment I turned away from the river to examine the house. The white black-shuttered farm was no more. Instead, a strange dark shape emerged — long and low — it fronted the river in points and angles like a monstrous accordion. As in a nightmare in which one returns to a familiar place only to find it radically altered, in the semidarkness I groped for the Riversedge I knew, reconstructing it: the kitchen would be here, the Italian urns there, the living room window here. But it was impossible; all my attempts ended in confrontation with that intrusive form, more like a grotesque dream sculpture than a house.

Later I had an opportunity to ask Ralph Ingersoll about his architect. "I really designed the house myself," he said. "It was built so that I could see the river from every room and hear it everywhere — loudly," he added. "I'm a little deaf." This was said in lordly fashion. The broad rushing Housatonic would be tamed to suit the aging emperor's whim. For his entertainment it would be turned into a court jester.

I shuddered. My vision was another one: two aging people had built a home for their declining years and, all unwittingly, they had admitted the River Lethe into every opening, recess and angle.

The Dream

*B*ecause of his paralyzed leg with its heavy brace George Gruntle had ordered a wheelchair to take him to the doctor's office aboard the QE 2. Instead, two stewards looking like orderlies in white uniforms arrived with a stretcher. Despite his protests, they lifted his tall uncoordinated body as though it were weightless and proceeded on their way. From his prone position Gruntle stared up at the fluorescent lights on the ceilings as he was carried through corridor after corridor, in and out of down-plunging elevators until they reached a subterranean realm lined in shining tiles. Gruntle grew quite dizzy and attempted to sit upright to avoid the glare, but he found that he was unable to move. He was reminded of the journey he had once made to an operating room. But then he had been half anesthetized and now, although it seemed years ago, he clearly recalled that he had been quite himself before the arrival of the orderlies. It was only that he had been having twinges of pain in his paralyzed leg that was usually numb. The stretcher bearers continued on their course — would this nightmare never end? At last they stopped before a door with a plaque that read: "Leopold Litvak, M.D." Gruntle was permitted to stand up, and still dazed and wavering he entered the doctor's office.

Dr. Litvak was seated at his desk; opposite him the regulation empty chair waited. It was all conventional except that the doctor was wearing a black silk mask over his eyes. Beneath it his beak nose, thin lips and the triangular shape of his face were emphasized. He motioned Gruntle to sit and without removing his mask he began to write his case history.

Gruntle told him about his useless leg and the twinges he had recently felt in it. But Dr. Litvak appeared more concerned with details about his flourishing pencil factory. Gruntle, with his elongated body, small bald head, pale structureless face and insignificant features bore a marked resemblance to his product: a pencil topped by its tiny standard eraser. He responded dutifully to all the doctor's questions; he had always had a feeling of awe for the medical profession, admiring and submissive. Gruntle, uncertain of love unless it was paid for, felt that his large doctor's bills entitled him to special attention and affection, and he surrendered to the physician with the trusting hopefulness of a child to a powerful father. Dr. Litvak had the power but the parental warmth was missing. He remained aloof, separated by the expanse of his desk.

As Gruntle responded to the probing interrogation on the accumulation of his wealth, he looked about him with increasing alarm. There was no one else in the office, no sign of a nurse or receptionist, not even a telephone or an intercommunication system. Instead of the usual diplomas the walls were hung with Surrealist drawings of medieval instruments of torture: the Iron Maiden and a guillotine that looked more clinical than historic. On the doctor's desk, in place of family photographs, there was a complicated sculpture made of nails, spikes and twisted wires. Gruntle shrank as far away from it as possible. At last the doctor rose and commanded him to undress. By this time, Gruntle, thoroughly unnerved, declared that he felt much better and would like to leave. But the exit had disappeared and without his volition his clothes dropped off him. His weak, shivering *body, clad only in the brace, rimless eyeglasses and a platinum watch was bared to the doctor, who, pressing a button, caused an examining table to arise. It was covered in black leather and had an irregular shape — extending in points and angles like a monstrous accordion — yet it was disturbingly familiar —*

When Gruntle was stretched out along its chilly surface, the doctor switched off the lights. For an instant there was total darkness. Then a piercing ray lit up the examining table and Gruntle saw that Dr. Litvak was without his mask. The intolerable glare was emanating from his eyes that appeared free from his face, two independent beacons with a separate existence of their own —

The doctor removed Gruntle's brace, his glasses and his wristwatch and started to prod his now totally nude defenseless body. His touch was surprisingly deft. After the examination, the patient, dressed, was replaced on the stretcher for the return journey. From nowhere the orderlies had reappeared.

"I will inform you about my findings at a later time," the doctor said.

"But I can't leave without my brace," Gruntle wailed.

"I am sending it to my foundry to be melted down and reshaped," the doctor answered. The mask was over his eyes and with his sleekly tailored black suit the effect was stylish and swashbuckling. For the first time George Gruntle noticed that Dr. Litvak had a limp and that the platinum watch on his wrist was identical to his own. The doctor bowed with ceremony and in his clipped slightly foreign accent he said, "Au revoir, Mr. Gruntle. I wish you continued success with your pencil factory."

He vanished suddenly, leaving a faint smell of sulfur in his wake. Before George Gruntle could inquire about the payment, he was borne upward — still helpless, still struggling, trapped in the meshes of an immaterial net.

THE COURTYARD
AND THE WAITING ROOM

ON MY WAY to Broadway to meet the writer Isaac Singer, I walk through that side street where the Café des Artistes and the Beaux Arts Apartments are. Like someone with blurred vision I try to single out number 15, which had once contained Francis Bradford's shadowy workshop, but all the façades merge, presenting a unified gray stone wall.

When I reach Broadway I wait for Singer outside the Tip Toe Inn. Here is another city within the multifaced oneness called New York. The pedestrians look foreign: refugee housewives laden with grocery bundles, others sporting New World finery minted on Seventh Avenue and elaborate, sprayed, tinted coiffures. Out of a subway exit a rabbinical figure emerges from underground, his long black skirts sweeping the dusty steps, his wide-brimmed hat, his grisly beard and sidelocks looking dusty and his eyes as hollow as open graves. A legless beggar holds out a tin cup and some yellow pencils, and an ownerless dog dodges among pedestrian legs, trotting purposefully as though he were not lost. A pair of transvestites undulate past me. No one pauses to notice them, although they are as blatant as the signs on the marquees outside the "skin flicks" — largely ignored also — except for an occasional lonely sailor or a sleazy traveling salesman. The midday crowd on Broadway goes by, blind alike to ugliness and sin, intent on the business of just another day.

Who is this crossing the wide avenue? He is of small stature, fair-complexioned and is wearing a long dark winter coat, although it is spring and the weather is warm. He is nearing seventy, yet he scuttles with the agility of a beetle. From under a felt hat his large pale blue eyes peer out, as darting as his gait. He is clutching a brown paper bag. It is Isaac Singer.

When he reaches me he bobs his head in an indication of an Old World bow. "I am not late, am I?" he asks. His English is flavored by his Yiddish accent, the same cadence that lingers in his translated stories and novels, giving them the blended richness of native brew. "I stopped on the way to buy bird food," he says, holding out the paper bag. Singer has an affinity for birds. "They are God's creatures too," he says. And he is a familiar sight on Broadway, scattering grain, surrounded by a congregation of bedraggled city pigeons.

After lunch we walk up Broadway to 86th Street where Singer lives. Our ritual does not vary but I still feel a stranger in a strange city. The Tip Toe Inn, quintessential Americana, had been a *lansleit* café and the cheesecake, rice pudding or stewed prunes I had watched Singer eating had been recognized details from his stories. Like a sightseer I regard the familiar eleven blocks between the restaurant and his apartment. We move quickly, and sometimes I am forced to break into a run to keep up with his scuttling pace. He is impatient to reach home to begin his translation. On the way he sometimes relates bits of a story he is working on: "It is called 'The Son from America' — he returns to the little town in Poland where he was born. He wants to bestow his American money on his simple parents and the village people. But they don't know how to use worldly gifts, they are contented to remain poor, chanting inside their synagogue, protected by their faith in God — I will not tell you what happens at the end — you will soon hear it — you will like it," Singer promises, while I gallop at his side as eager as he to get there.

Singer's apartment building is a relic constructed during the nineteenth century. Once a luxury building, it is a large, solid rectangle enclosing a sunless courtyard. Now somewhat shabby, it looks like a fortress or, perhaps, a converted prison. Singer once told me that he chose it because the courtyard reminded him of his childhood home in Warsaw. We open a bastillelike gate and cross the yard. Our footsteps echo, we are alone in the deserted area.

Outside his door he stoops to pick up his mail: Yiddish periodicals, magazines on extrasensory perception (he is a fanatical subscriber) and his fan letters. The interior is spacious, a long obscure foyer, living room and dining room furnished in conventional, continental bourgeoisie style by Alma, Singer's wife, who comes from Munich. He appears a transient here. Two rooms, rarely visited, are particularly his. The study where he composes is crammed with manuscripts and old newspapers. But the disorder is only apparent, the flurry is a sign of power — it is like the eye of the storm. In the bedroom two parakeets fly free; the door of their cage is always open. A male and a female, they look like enamel birds, electric blue and parrot green. But I know that they are a poor substitute for the original: Matzoth.

The story of Matzoth tells something significant but not definable about Singer. One summer morning as he was sitting at the kitchen table by the window open to the courtyard, he wished for a companion. Immediately, as if in answer, a parakeet flew inside. "As soon as I saw him I knew we would be friends. God had sent him to me. He was an old soul." Seeing them together I could understand. Matzoth would alight on Singer's bald pate and Singer, holding very still and rolling his large pale blue eyes upward, would converse with the bird in a special voice reserved just for him. "Say something, Matzoth," he would coax. "I am listening." The bird would chirp away. Seeing them like this I could not help noticing their likeness: Singer's small round face with his Semitic nose and wise eyes was repeated in avian terms by Matzoth's tiny aquiline profile and the uncanny intelligence of his expression. "Talk, Matzoth," and, turning to me, "No, don't go away, he is about to say something." While waiting I leafed through the case-history books on demonic possession on Singer's desk. Matzoth continued to peep. At last Singer said, "He has spoken." "What did he say?" He said, " 'Case history,' " Singer answered. With a twinkle and a shrug he released me and the bird flew off his perch on the domed forehead. "There are more things in this world than you and I can understand," said Singer. A few years later after Matzoth's sudden appearance, he disappeared on another hot summer morning. In spite of the heat it had been ordered that the windows must always be shut when Matzoth was loose, but on this day Alma had been careless, for the window on the courtyard had been left ajar and through it Matzoth departed as abruptly as he had entered. Singer, frantic, placed lost notices in the newspapers, searched the streets, inquired of neighbors, but Matzoth had vanished forever. "It was God's will. He came and he went." But he could not conceal his grief. "These two," he would say about the replacements, "are foolish creatures." The frivolous pair would dart about the bedroom, pecking here, perching there, clinging with their twiglike, sharp claws to the ceiling, heads downward. "They are not old souls like Matzy," said Singer.

Singer takes off his overcoat, hangs it in the closet in the foyer and scurries to his armchair in the living room from which he dictates his translations. I sit on the hotel-striped satin sofa with a pad on my knees and scramble, as on our walks, to keep pace with him. Through the years the stories proliferate, alien characters have become familiar: Yentl, Beyle, Mier, the eunuch, Zalman the glazier, Zeinvel, Zeitl, Itche Godl, Getsl, the magic rebbes, the youths in their study house, the women in the ritual bath. Place names, still unpronounceable, have become old friends: Rejowiec, Shidlovtse, Radom, Kielce, Krasnobrod and Bilgoray. My role is that of grammarian, enabling me to change the tense of a verb, or alter its position, but, in truth, I have become the listener of old and he the proverbial storyteller. When at last he lays aside *The Jewish Daily Forward* with a serialized Yiddish version of his tale, or a manuscript on loose scraps of paper covered in his small illegible handwriting, I beg to know the ending — what will happen? But Singer puts me off with "We finish it next time — you will see — "

At intervals during a session he jumps up to answer the telephone, a confirmation of a lecture engagement or another fan. He returns to the armchair and the dictation is resumed as though there had been no interruption; his concentration is continuous. And in his work his vision makes the universe whole, all contradictions reconciled: Old World — new world, the Torah and the cabala, the saintliness of human beings and their swinishness.

I can still remember the first story he translated in this

fashion in my presence. It was called "Henne Fire" and its subject was a witchlike woman, as dark and emaciated as a charred bone. She was an incendiary who caused flames to spring up wherever she might be. Singer told me that he had glimpsed the model for this imaginative creation when he was ten years old, through a keyhole view into the court of his father, the Rabbi. He had kept it in the storage house of memory to be used some fifty years later. But in the prominent sharp eyes of the adult the small boy's curiosity peers out. And what the child learned in his father's court the man proclaims today. Through the many strands of his tales runs a single obsession: one must never forsake the ancient faith of the Hebrew forebears. So we sit side by side and far apart. We are like remote cousins with contrasting nationalities and family customs: The mystic Eastern European ghetto Jew and the wealthy New York City Jew of German descent, atheistically reared. We never cease to marvel, inwardly, at our differences while, at the same time, sharing our consanguinity.

Singer puts down his manuscript. "We will finish it next time."

"How does it end?"

"You will see."

The session is over for the day. My fingers are cramped yet I am not tired, I would like more. Downstairs the courtyard is still deserted. But in my mind's eye it has broken into seething activity: the Yeshiva boys, the shopkeepers, the glaziers, the midwives, the town gossips, the beadles jostle one another and the air is filled with the archaic singsong of the Yiddish language. From a window in his father's house the rabbi's little boy surveys the scene. The memory of it empowers the magic lantern eyes of the writer, Isaac Singer, to populate an empty New York City courtyard with the vanished life of the Warsaw ghetto. I pass through the bastillelike entrance and the harsh reality of Broadway is like a dream.

*

Shameful and hard to understand now was the remoteness of many New York City Jews from the Holocaust in Europe. I was an adolescent at that time, endlessly concerned with my own existence. The gas chambers, the corpses and Hitler's ranting proclamation were no more than horrible images on a screen or bloodless statistics in a newspaper. My only acquaintance out of that unreal inferno was a Berlin doctor who arrived here in the midthirties with a letter of introduction to my parents. Strangely, he always appeared to me as the very essence of the Teutonic, a calm, philosophical man who reminded me of Hans Sachs in Wagner's opera *Die Meistersinger*. He was short and broad, barrel shaped, with a large head and thick fair hair. His mouth was marred by an old dueling scar from Heidelberg student days. He was a half Jew and he arrived on our shores accompanied by his Aryan wife, Rosa, also a doctor, and his dimwitted spinster sister-in-law, Elsa. Rosa was fat with a brick red face and a clumsy bun of flaxen hair; she looked like a village innkeeper but for her owlish eyes behind thick scholarly glasses. Elsa kept house for her sister and brother-in-law with German thoroughness. Everything was shining and scoured, and she cooked the heavy meals they all enjoyed, hare, venison, potato pancakes, which they washed down with beer.

When this trio turned up at our Sunday lunches I did not connect them with the plight of the Jews. Rather, as I observed them around the table, alien in our midst, they reminded me of the solid fronts of the houses of Nuremberg, the clock towers, gabled roofs and storks' nests I'd seen on my childhood travels. But my mother, always sensitive to other peoples' miseries, in her generosity, making them her own, was the only one to offer true asylum to Doctor Muller and his family.

For this reception, his devotion to her and his admiration were to endure. With hindsight, it has even occurred to me that he might have been in love with her. But the thought of a parent inspiring romance is repugnant to the child. I recall a summer afternoon in Paris, when my mother was accompanying me to the Tuileries where I was to meet school friends. I see the celluloid boats we launched in the basin that was as large as a pond in the center of the geometric alleys. Surrounded by French children, we listened to their nimble tongues and the exotic timbre of their voices as we watched the wavering shadows made by their hoops on the wide dusty paths. My mother and their father sat side by side on rented chairs. They formed a pretty picture in the dappled light and shade of the park — an Impressionist portrait handed down to me. But the expression in their eyes, furtive, tentative, excited, came to me later. That afternoon in the Tuileries Gardens the faces of my mother and her companion were blanks before my eyes.

Ernst Muller shared our board, and he was a frequent visitor in our home, but I was as incurious about his present as I was about his past. Eventually he became my physician, after he had assisted, unavailing, at my mother's untimely death and years later at my father's terminal illness. I used to think that his kindness and special attention to my father also dated from that earlier hospitality. On those cozy visits, after office hours, he looked much the same, only his blond hair was graying and he was more portly and deliberate. He still retained his German accent, and the Heidelberg dueling scar was as visible as ever. He and my father drank a nightcap of beer together and reminisced about former days.

Doctor Muller's office on Park Avenue was fashionable, the waiting room wood-paneled, the desk in the inner sanctum large, the examining room well appointed. Rosa acted as his technician, but I always fancied that her chief duty was to arrange, each week, the little vase of assorted flowers that came from the Mullers' rock garden in Peekskill. Ernst, Rosa and Elsa were proud of their country place located in a hilly section of northern Westchester. Perhaps it reminded them of Bavaria, because they clung to it and did not return to Europe, even for a visit. Despite his repeated invitations, I never saw the house, but it was well represented by that constantly renewed frail bouquet on the office desk.

I would sit in the waiting room, preoccupied with my own minor ills, hardly aware of the others also attending their summons within. Stale magazines passed the time. But I did notice that many of the patients had a shabby, self-effacing appearance. One day when I was with the doctor, he conducted a protracted telephone conversation in German. Apologizing afterward for the delay, he explained that for some years he had been assessing the restitution claims of concentration camp survivors. Examining them for permanent physical and psychological damage, he spent long hours compiling voluminous paperwork in connection with each case. I looked at Doctor Muller, sturdy, well fed and established here, and I wondered if part of him could still identify with those maimed lives in need of his help. Was it guilt, thankfulness, the German side of him begging pardon of the Jewish that caused him to donate his services free to those humble claimants, while he compensated by sending exorbitant bills to his rich American patients?

Even after I had identified these foreign visitors, I continued to view them as ghosts and I seemed to be looking through their transparencies to the dark-paneled oak of the waiting room walls. Two composite portraits remain in memory: a frail gentleman in a tattered stained tweed coat several sizes too large sitting with his knees pressed together, his chin on his bony hand resting on a jaunty cane, staring ahead, unseeing, now and then a racking cough threatens to shatter this uncertain assemblage, a scarecrow in the wind. A woman adjusts her mangy fur piece, the beady artificial eyes of the fox more alive than hers; she wears darned white cotton gloves. I knew that under the dilapidated gentility of outer garments there was a number branded into wasted flesh and that mute patience was a cover for seering, indelible memories. When the door of the office opened and one of these apparitions was ushered in or out, there would be a low salutation or an attempt at a cheerful goodby, overtaken by the reassuring voice of Doctor Muller, speaking his native tongue — still the calm, kindly Hans Sachs of our first meeting.

He is dead now and I do not know if those ghostly survivors of the Holocaust live on. For me, they had been less flesh and blood than the population in an empty courtyard created by the genius of Isaac Singer.

Last winter while my husband and I were vacationing in Miami, Singer, who now lives there part of the year, asked me to work on a story with him. Broadway had yielded place to Collins Avenue and a new bright white condominium, heavily carpeted, with a plastic sculpture in the lobby. It was a strange home for him and I felt nostalgia for the shabby rectangular fortress and its sunless courtyard. The elevator mounted to dizzy heights and my husband and I were disgorged into a compact, light apartment, the entire dwelling no larger than the obscure foyer at 86th Street. It was sparsely furnished and I wondered what we would use instead of Singer's armchair and the striped sofa. After a hospitable coffee klatch with rich cakes, served by Alma in elaborate Munich style, Singer, always impatient to return to his stories, said, "Now we get to work."

He and I moved out to a balcony, a small perch overlooking miles of empty beach, sea and flawless blue sky. The inhabitants of the condominium preferred to swim in a crowded, heated freshwater pool. The lavish display of seascape took me by surprise as the high-rise buildings on Collins Avenue, asserting the synthetic advantages of city living had hidden nature, reducing it to no more than a neglected backyard. "How beautiful!" I exclaimed. "One would never guess this existed here."

Singer bobbed his head as though acknowledging a personal compliment, but he quickly sat down with his back to the view. Was it indifference or the politeness of a host? He was wearing a dark suit, as if there had been no transplantation from New York City to Miami Beach. The loose pages of his manuscript covered with his small illegible writing in Yiddish were the same, as were the yellow pad on my knees, the rapid dictation. As usual, I rushed to keep pace with him. But my eyes kept straying to the extravagant sea spread over his shoulder below until his tale took possession of me. Once again I was back among the pious rabbis, the *lansleit* in the cafeterias, the Yiddish journalists, the yeshiva students, the housewives baking the Sabbath loaves, the miracles, the dybbuks — reaching me through the lips of the immemorial storyteller. The courtyard that had reminded Singer of his boyhood Warsaw home was, after all, an unnecessary stage set, no more vital than the beach in Miami. Isaac Singer's world, the world of the historic Jew, does not have its true existence among the perishable phenomena of things in space. From biblical recording to the events of contemporary days, the Diaspora, enacted again and again, has made the Jew a transient in all places of the earth. Yet he endures. Singer is a link in a chain celebrating in words the continuation of a people in abiding Time.

The Dream

*L*eopold Litvak, culture professional, held his classes in the main lounge. He had full attendance and the young millionaires and their wives arrived promptly like conscientious schoolchildren: Johnsons, Newmans, Oberdorfers, George Gruntle and the others. Pamela Mellow was present without Marty, who invariably napped after his heavy midday meal.

In place of the plush furniture and potted plants, rows of desks had appeared. They were not made of the usual wood, scarred and etched by idle hands; the scholars on board the QE 2 were fitted inside cages of steel chairs attached to steel lecterns.

Jack and Erica Baker sat in the front row. Jack headed his own advertising firm founded on his wife's family fortune in canned food products. He was a serious, plodding, unimaginative man capable of hard work. His literal mind allowed him to accept unquestioningly the slick slogans and visual tricks of Madison Avenue, a young benefactor to the "writers" and "artists" in his organization. He was comely in an obvious shallow way, with smooth olive skin and sheer eyes. Apparently uninfluenced by the ponytails and Afros worn by many of his contemporaries, his black hair was neatly clipped. Erica was handsome also. A large athletic girl from the northwest, she loved to ski and reminisce about team sports at the Madeira School.

She had a close-fitting cap of blond curls and the features of a Greek head on a coin. Wide shouldered and narrow hipped, in her casual pantsuits she resembled a proper Princeton fullback, but her mouth, painted iridescent mauve pink, was heavy, sensuous and shapely. She was given to telling gory anecdotes about hospital experiences and accidents. Disaster and bloodshed were her natural element.

Now she listened to Leopold Litvak with fascination. Although a copy of Crime and Punishment lay on the table in front of him, his recital was of his own making, autobiography or fiction — it was impossible to say. It began with an account of his escape from Poland and Russia, the fantastic mingling with the mundane until a Grimms' tale was transformed into the ordinary and the ingenuity of one man into the supernatural. He had no notes, and his piercing eyes searched the complacent faces beneath him; he chose his words as though they were components in an alchemist's experiment. He stood on a dais, slender and upright in his tight bold plaid suit; behind him, for no apparent purpose, a blackboard was chalked in Latin calligraphy. But his story was up to date, delivered in a nasal, high-pitched, controlled voice that was like a lash — "I arrived in New York City in nineteen fifty-seven. Although I had already sold some stories in English to the 'little magazines,' I didn't have a dime to my name. I accepted menial jobs: grease monkey, car-park, hospital orderly, even men's lavatory attendant. One day I walked uptown from the garage where I was employed. It was lunchtime and my stomach was growling from emptiness. A heavy spring rain plastered my cheap suit but walking the streets of Manhattan was my pleasure. Under a canopy outside a fashionable restaurant some wealthy women were waiting for the doorman to summon their cars. They were imperious and overdressed and I looked them over like so much merchandise. The doorman was receiving large tips but the women were growing impatient. A limousine drew up to the curb. Sitting beside the chauffeur was an enormous, cadaverous, fierce, furred silhouette. A woman weighted in diamond and gold jewelry detached herself from the group and entered the limousine. At once the shaggy wolfhound leaped onto the back seat, covering his mistress in a rough embrace. What rites are carried on at home, in privacy, I wondered, and I substituted my own body for the hound's in the comfort of the upholstered seat."

Erica Baker stirred restlessly. She felt powerfully drawn to Leopold Litvak. He continued, "The rain did not let up. The doorman under his umbrella was having a difficult time finding taxis for the remaining diners. His whistle was bleak and ineffectual. A stout woman standing beneath the marquee caught my eye. She was past middle age and I could guess that hidden in her silk dress her body would be ample yet unawakened. She had a delicate face on which traces of the popular pampered debutante still lingered. I could see myself as her companion in the foreign cities of the world. But at night I would leave her sleeping in the hotel room of our suite (it would have the best view of the Grand Canal, the Spanish Steps or the Place Vendôme) to explore the back streets where unmasked crime flourishes. This is where I find the raw material for my books."

Erica glanced at Jack, who appeared to be dozing. He was such a bore, kindly, but unsatisfactory as a lover. Conventional and hasty, he shrank from her more imaginative manipulations. As she listened to Litvak she determined that she must manage to be alone with him after the lecture.

Litvak continued, "The blond woman drove off too, and I directed my steps toward the Queensborough Bridge. Its complicated, awkward structure has always attracted me. I like its skeletal towers and mighty steel spans. After dark it looks like a ghostly castle, a bejeweled jail. The rain had stopped and I felt *resilient and sure-footed. I stood on the bridge, and the sky-scraper silhouette of Manhattan rose before me. It is menacing to some, but I thought of it as a challenge. As a child I learned to control my destiny. Now I exulted in power: I would prevail — alone. To be self-sufficient is to be free.*

Leopold Litvak paused, observed his audience and said, "Ladies and gentlemen, I have some pills here that I usually use as a stimulus during my classes." He stepped down from the dais and distributed the drug among the young millionaires and their wives. Many accepted as though under hypnosis, a few refused. George Gruntle swallowed eagerly; perhaps this man could help him in some way, the ship doctor having failed.

Litvak resumed his position on the dais, his raven's head framed by the blackboard with its magic, medieval lettering. By this time his students had begun to be queasy — was the ship pitching or rolling? They could not feel it; perhaps the sumptuous luncheon buffet had been tainted, or the liquor.

"Ladies and gentlemen, I have administered a mild emetic. It is my custom — "

There was a loud splash as George Gruntle vomited a lumpy yellowish torrent over his desk. He looked mildly startled, as though it were happening to someone else. Members of the audience tried to get out but discovered that they were locked in their steel vises. They hammered on the desktops, shouted and cursed. Erica had no desire to escape.

"It is sometimes necessary to be shaken up a bit," said Litvak and, ignoring the occasional retching and the shouts, he proceeded and quiet was restored. By this time the definitions of Erica's identity were blurred and she felt herself merging with the blond woman in Litvak's discourse.

At the close of the session everybody seemed to have forgotten the professor's bizarre methods. Released, the young millionaires and their wives left the lounge in good order. Only Erica *lingered in the vacated room with its empty rattraps. Litvak was approaching her. She kneeled before him embracing his legs. Her shapely lips, tinted frosty mauve like the petals of a morning glory, parted to receive his aroused organ. Instead, her mouth was filled with the shell-wood hardness of a bird's beak. It reached down into her throat. She gagged and struggled, not realizing that nightmares terminate themselves. Leopold Litvak, culture professional, was nowhere.*

THE HOUSE OF LETTERS

ON THE FIRST VISIT to Wellfleet on Cape Cod the summer
following Edmund Wilson's death we found the house the
same yet strangely altered. His widow, Elena, ushered my
husband and me into the wing that had been Wilson's
kingdom consisting of library, bedroom (once a woodshed
and added in recent years during his illness) and bathroom.
In the library not one volume had been disturbed. They
were all well cared for, yet they looked dim and recessive.
The low ceilinged and meandering book-lined workroom,
once the heart of the house, had been abandoned. Taine,
Proust, Michelet, Tolstoi, Chekhov, Pushkin, Dostoevski,
Gogol, Turgenev (the latter in the original Russian), Dickens, Renan, Balzac, Dante, the grotesquely erotic drawings
of Aubrey Beardsley, and Fuseli — philosophy, history, literary criticism — all Wilson's lifelong friends stood faith-
fully in place on their shelves.

Light filtered from a corner window near the desk. Over
his work chair a sign in Hebrew read: "Let us be strong,
stronger still stronger," a chant used by Talmudic scholars
exhorting further efforts. Wilson had come across the lines
while doing research in Israel for *The Scrolls from the Dead*

Sea. A stuffed owl bearing an uncanny resemblance to Wilson was now the recipient of the ancient message. And in the village cemetery just beyond the house a simple tombstone under a great shade tree is engraved with the same phrase. As it had accompanied Edmund Wilson, alive, now it seemed to be following him in death. We were aware that the temerity of our toothbrushes in the bathroom, our open suitcase packed with bathing suits and jeans in the bedroom, and our appropriation of the adjacent library would not transform this wing into guest quarters. The absence of a presence barred the way.

My introduction to the Edmund Wilsons and to the house in Wellfleet took place in 1950. Of that visit nothing remains but the recollection of sitting in the little flower garden situated outside the "blue room," always especially Elena's. On this August afternoon we were awaiting the arrival of Edmund Wilson, who was in Boston for the rehearsal of his new play, *The Little Blue Light.* My husband had just become his publisher and I was eager for this first meeting. At that time Wilson was in his late fifties, but I imagined him already venerable, indelibly etched against his reputation, an American Gibbon or a Samuel Johnson. I pictured him like a central character out of Molière, an intimidating eccentric seated center stage with his bandaged gouty foot upraised, surrounded by a group of minions ready to execute his every testy demand.

Elena Wilson came from an aristocratic European background: a German father, heir to the von Mumm champagne fortune, and a White Russian mother. Her childhood had been divided between a formal town house outside of Frankfurt, and hotel suites in Paris and Switzerland, and it was punctuated by visits to international resorts fashionable around the time of the First World War. After Hit-

ler's takeover she had left Europe and her family, arriving
in the United States, armed with the courage and idealism
that would continue to serve her through the years. In her
New England garden that looked like a patchwork apron attached to the early nineteenth-century Cape Cod house, she
was far removed from the *hôtels splendides* of Biarritz, Davos
and Marienbad. Yet now she belonged here. I observed
her; a tall woman, slightly stooped, her posture reminded
me of a stem, flexible but resilient. Her face was lovely and
blooming. She looked more Teutonic than Russian: casual
bobbed wavy blond hair, gentian blue eyes, rosy skin
somewhat weathered from the salt air of her adopted land, a
sensitive nose with flared nostrils and a generous mouth,
slightly puckered as though she were about to laugh, cry or
pronounce one of those German words that require oral cal-
isthenics. But French was Elena's first language and she
spoke the correct English taught by governesses, tinged
with a foreign inflection. She was wearing a faded checked
gingham shirtwaist dress, her sunburned legs were
scratched from berry picking and dotted with mosquito
bites, her large solid feet were bare. Yet there was about
her an air of regality. The Wilsons' two-year-old daughter,
Helen, playing near her mother, had been born when Elena
was over forty and Edmund twelve years older. The baby
was sturdy, with features already firm and determined.
She regarded us with owlish omniscience. There were
other children by the Wilsons' previous marriages. We
were discussing a forthcoming book of collected essays,
when suddenly Elena broke off to exclaim, "Edmund is approaching!"

I kept looking down the country road that ran close to the
house but the occasional passing automobile did not stop.
At last I asked, "Didn't I hear you say that Mr. Wilson was
arriving?"

"Oh, he won't be here for another forty minutes."

"But I thought—"

"I only meant that I felt his presence," she answered in her deep voice with its foreign inflection. "I know these things. I have a kind of sixth sense—" This was said quite simply as a statement of fact. A touch of other-worldliness completes my first impression of Elena. Contact with the mystical is as natural to her as the company of the crowned heads of Europe must have been to her parents, vacationing at summer spas or winter ski resorts.

Edmund Wilson did indeed arrive at the minute predicted by his wife. But that initial meeting is unclear in memory, as though I had been trying to discern him through a glare — projected not by the "blue light" of his own drama but by Elena's extrasensory prologue to his entrance on stage. That afternoon belonged to her; after that Wilson generally took over. And I never again set foot inside the small garden attached like an apron to the blue room. It became a picture behind a glass door: a daguerreotype, idyllic but flat, a background against which we were posed for an instant: Elena, Helen, my husband, I and that blurred likeness of Edmund Wilson—the progenitors of our later selves.

In many New England country houses the kitchen is situated so that it constitutes a central gathering place. The Wilsons' confronted the visitor as soon as he entered the door. In all seasons we lingered there in informal sociability around the perimeter of the oilcloth-covered table on which Elena would have placed a jug of rambler roses, zinnias, autumn leaves or a sprig of pine. She was an early riser, moving about downstairs at daybreak, and when we descended, the ashtrays in the kitchen would already be filled with the stubs of her morning cigarettes. She was a proficient but absent-minded cook, plodding back and forth between range and table, her feet still bare, her scrubbed face devoid of make-up.

Now Edmund Wilson entered the picture. He would appear late, sometimes still in pajamas that had an oddly formal look. Elena would serve him a special meal in her distracted but efficient manner — pancakes or Irish oatmeal — which he ate with appetite while delivering vehement opinions on the Russian novel, new and old — or extolling the fascination of a language he was currently studying: Hebrew, Russian, modern Greek or Hungarian. My portrait in advance had not been altogether incorrect. In his fifties Edmund Wilson did look old, but in a crusty solid fashion that one felt would be more lasting than mere youthfulness. For the twenty years I saw him, a few times each year — until his final illness — he did not change. In the beginning I found him intimidating: his snappish comments, his talent for utter silence that was even more disconcerting, his explosive laughter that sounded as though it were erupting over obstacles, like a dammed waterfall forcing its way between heavy boulders. In the morning he joined us around the kitchen table, but he was the unmistakable potentate. He would at times unbend with my husband, who could call forth most frequently that eruptive laugh, and Wilson's faith in him, blunt but unswerving, endured. In his bathrobe and pajamas he did resemble that cranky eighteenth-century character I had anticipated. Short and plump, his presence was nonetheless impressive, his face owlish, his features grown smaller in proportion to the expansion of his jowls. He had round, protruding, claret-colored eyes under hooded lids — the eyes of the perpetual scholar most at ease when cast down upon the page of a book. Yet when he raised them to the world about him, nothing escaped their reddish brown stare. His nose was pointed and inquisitive, his mouth above several chins was compressed, more censorious than his eyes. His hands were small, doll-like, as though belonging to a lesser man.

My husband and he would have much to talk about. Later in the day when they shut themselves into Wilson's study, Elena and I would go for walks along the beach, accompanied by the current Wilson dog. The first, addressed by Edmund as "old flea-bag," had been a furry mop of uncertain shape and breed. He had been succeeded by "Brown," for the most part, boxer. In November, the dunes were like bare giant shoulders exposed to the chilly crystalline glint of the sea and a flawless blue sky. Our footprints were insignificant on the expanse of smooth sand and Elena's ease alone with nature communicated itself to me.

In the early days lunch and dinner were taken in the dining room. Later, when Edmund was ill and Elena's burdens had increased, the kitchen served for all meals. The dining room was conventional American Colonial but Edmund, ceremonious in the observance of holidays; anniversaries, Easter, Christmas, birthdays — not even overlooking April Fool's and Valentine's Day, had contributed ornaments that stood out in the homespun décor like orchids growing among wildflowers. I remember, in particular, an epergne made of mauve frosted glass that might have graced the salon of one of the hostesses of Marcel Proust.

I rarely entered the adjacent drawing room. It was obscure, furnished with authentic American antiques: a black horsehair sofa, a maple desk honeycombed with caches, a table covered in green baize. This room did not seem to belong either to Elena or Edmund. It was the departed spirit of Mary McCarthy, its former mistress, that lurked in the dusky corners. An authentic New England drawing room, correct and quaint, it might be prized by an outlander from the raw northwest.

In the Wilson home the guest bedrooms are reached by ladderlike stairs. White-painted wooden doors are still bolted by the original iron latches and floor and ceilings tilt at dizzy angles. The rooms are numerous but small and unadorned, but the windows hold pleasant segments of rural views: a white-shingle extension of the house topped by a weather vane, a patch of tangled field, an old oak, the narrow rugged dirt path separating the main house from the crooked front steps of the "cottage." Everywhere there was a trace of salty dampness and the nostalgic smell of old country houses: a mixture of recent scrubbings and the unmistakable residual odor of longevity, as though soap and water had been joined to ineradicable dust and rot. All the extra bedrooms were repositories for a copious overflow of books. Here, stacked on hand-built shelves, bureau tops, night tables and window benches, were to be found the leftovers of bygone research: the Depression years, Indian tribes of upstate New York, Russian literature and the Russian Revolution, the Civil War. Their bindings rubbed shoulders with discarded review copies and the works of old friends now outmoded: Dawn Powell, Waldo Frank, Louis Bromfield, Zelda Fitzgerald, Dorothy Parker, Sinclair Lewis, John Dos Passos. In this setting they, like the odor in the guest bedrooms, had an antiquated lure.

Many hours were spent in Elena's sunny "blue room." Perhaps I thought of it as hers because of its color that complemented her eyes in a symphony of blues ranging from royal to delphinium to pale cerulean. I was mesmerized by a small painting on the wall: a wooden door opening on to the dunes and a clear sky, executed in minute detail, it appeared to be a real aperture in the cozy room, as actual as the garden beyond the glass door. Elena would curl up on the powder blue couch. At night she would be wearing a long loose blue robe, her bare feet tucked up under its hem. Edmund ensconced himself in a certain armchair nearest the entrance to his study. In the "blue room," he always seemed a visitor, albeit an illustrious one. His conversation dominated. At these times Elena was mostly silent, but her bright blue eyes were lively and her generous mouth always appeared on the verge of laughter, crying, or pronouncing that tongue-twisting German word foreign to the rest of us. Edmund's monologues, like his mirth, were spasmodic, delivered with a slight stammer that added emphasis. His face would grow suffused in apoplectic red, brought on by his vehemence and by the succession of drinks that marked the evening hours with the steadfastness of the ticking of the grandfather's clock in the unused drawing room.

Other visitors were rare. Sometimes Helen, now a teen-ager, was there with a group of friends. Elena kept casual open house for young people who were drawn to her. She respected their point of view and they admired the un-self-consciousness of her youthful spirit. Edmund remained obdurately the "grand old man." He held himself aloof from his children and their companions, but I am certain that no detail escaped the observation of his hooded eyes. From his chair, clapping his doll-like hands, he called out imperiously, "Bring in the 'hippies'!" And Helen and her friends would troop into the blue room, court jesters for his entertainment. The girls wore floor-length printed cotton skirts, T-shirts over free-bobbing breasts and handmade dangling jewelry. They looked like Gypsy fortune tellers. The boys, long haired, in picturesquely patched jeans, re-sembled Greenwich Village saints. College students and dropouts, they consecrated themselves to crude carpentry and the baking of coarse whole-grained bread. Helen's features were bold and clear-cut; she had heavy bones and large gray eyes like the women from Picasso's "classical" period. But her expression, honest and penetrating, was her father's, and her young lips were molded in the shape of his eloquent severity. Harlequins on parade, Helen and her friends presented themselves before Edmund, and like Old King Cole, enthroned on his chair, he passed them all in review. The solemn humorless "generation gap" had been converted into a cheerful extravaganza: a mock clash between the exuberance of youth in confrontation with the self-respecting authority of age.

The blue room contained portraits and snapshots of Elena's family: her granddaughters by the son of her previous marriage, her mother pompadoured or in a large hat trimmed with milliner's roses, wearing a boned high-collared shirtwaist or draped in a boa. Of Edmund's family there were no pictures. It seemed to me that he carried his heritage and traditions on his person. Behind his intellect that had penetrated in wide arcs so many foreign places and people stood the indigenous New Jersey and upstate New York Calvinist ancestors — shadows stubbornly clinging to light.

In recent years some new paintings had made their appearance on the walls of the house in Wellfleet. Angular, uncompromising portraits and bright still lifes — they were the work of Helen Wilson. Last spring my husband and I dined with her in her studio loft, the size of a skating rink, in New York City. But her paintings stood out undwarfed. There were self-portraits without a tinge of prettiness, Helen's classical features caught in moods of cool detachment, and likenesses of members of her circle of friends, also painted without mercy, magnified heads against grounds of brilliant patchwork quilt patterns. I recognized the paintings of goblets, eggs, sugar bowls, shells, vegetables and fruits that I had seen before in the house at Wellfleet. In the stretch of the loft-studio a dining table, some miscellaneous borrowed chairs and a bed were reduced to insignificance. Helen was wearing a burlap robe, and with her straight Joan of Arc hair she looked like a priestess. This was Greenwich Village 1975 and it occurred to me that history in its circular fashion was repeating itself. Helen had the leading role that evening in a situation recalling the one enacted years earlier by Edmund Wilson, just out of Princeton, caught up and converted by the lure of the arts and of free love in the Village circa 1920. After dinner, consisting of a quiche, a loaf of homemade black bread, plenty of red wine and a salad culled by Helen from the stalls of Chinatown, she brought out some old family photographs for us to see. Among them was a wedding group: the bride and groom were Elena's parents surrounded by a large formal gathering in front of a home whose dimensions and glass port-cochère entrance vied in opulence with Berlin's Hotel Adlon. The groom was wearing Elena's face and the face of her son. He was tall and slender and also stooped like a stalk in the wind. Everyone looked long-lasting, yet they were all dead now. The photograph had found its way to this Greenwich Village loft. Helen's guests, the young harlequins, gazed in amazement at the richly dressed, pompous figures. Yet, mysteriously, Helen, one of them, was also connected to that buried scene. My husband and I bid good night to our hostess and descended the clanking iron stairs, seven flights to street level. A gentle rain had begun to fall. The grimy sidewalk littered with trash cans was deserted, but I felt companioned by the phantom of the young new-Bohemian, Edmund Wilson, and the members of that wedding party. The American writer and the off-spring of the European bride and groom, widely separated, innocent of their fate, were to be joined at some future point through the intricate weavings of chance and time.

Between Boston and Wellfleet an early winter blizzard had begun and soon we were shrouded in layers of cotton batting. Our rented car crawled and skidded on the deserted throughway. Now and then the twin glow of headlights, seemingly detached from any vehicle, approached us out of the horizonless universe. Nature had triumphed and the airport we had just left had grown remote in time and space. When finally we arrived Edmund and Elena gave us warm welcome. The snow was flattering to the old house, merging patches of shabbiness into a study in white and replacing the noise of cars (on what used to be the country road) with a dense hush.

But it was inside the library that we found a real haven from the storm — or, perhaps, its ally, because here also technocracy was locked out. In the world of Wilson's study he reigned, magician-king, fierce enemy to the machine age. An inhabitant of Cape Cod, reared in New Jersey, rooted in Talcottville, New York, Wilson was an unclassifiable type: a northern agrarian. And his bookshelves were a bulwark defying the ugly giant spawned by the Industrial Revolution.

By this time I had grown accustomed to his impatient bark, his explosive laughter, as well as to his long silences. I discovered in the formidable intellectual a core of childlike wonder. All his life Wilson had been an amateur magician, delighting in the staging of magic and puppet shows for the young, and I suspected that at those times he was both the performer and the beholder. Also, the clear-headed eighteenth-century rationalist was often tempted into foggier regions. Wilson went on with his study of religious meta-physics, the seductive snake in the garden of pure reason. He would splutter and inveigh against "ignorant superstitions" and the evils of the Catholic Church, but his shelves were filled with many well-thumbed tomes on religions of all times from every part of the world.

The storm continued and we were contented in the library. It was an enclosed room, almost windowless, yet the books were openings leading everywhere. And Wilson was an ideal guide, at once pedagogue and scholar. At this period he was rereading Dickens, for him a much-repeated occupation. On the morning of his death a dog-eared copy of *The Mystery of Edwin Drood* was found by his bedside. My experience with Dickens consisted mainly of childhood acquaintance with *David Copperfield* and *Oliver Twist* and later reading out loud to my young restless son, enveloped in steam from the croup kettle and accompanied by its medicinal gurgle. I was ignorant enough to say to Edmund Wilson that Dickens was not to my taste. An explosion followed. Wilson remained seated, but he looked as though he were in the thick of battle. He did not raise his voice, but it became a cannon directed at the density of my ignorance. "Have you ever read *Little Dorrit?*" he stammered. "No — well go home and do it!" His violence was ignition as was the discourse that followed. That winter I wallowed in Dickens. In a belated awakening I read all of it and nothing else. But I was constantly mindful, too, of Wilson in his library on a snowy afternoon. I recalled the Hebrew saying near his desk, the stuffed owl and the multitude of volumes opening out upon discovery.

As he grew old, irrascible and ill, his appearances in the other rooms became rarer and more brief. In his study he would examine a picture book of grotesque statuary, a garden of perverted shapes outside a Renaissance Italian palace. The Beasts of Bomarzo were favorites of his, representing the utmost audacity of the twisted imagination. Once he looked up and remarked wistfully, "I never saw all of it. The steps were too much for me." But the opened book was restorative. Wilson was approaching eighty: more bald — at times fatter, at other times, alarmingly shrunken, his steps tottering, a glass of whiskey, an indispensable crutch. A prisoner in the house, he could no longer travel; even walks on the beach had become too strenuous, and he was dependent on the gentle routine of afternoon drives with Elena as chauffeur. Yet at moments in the library, through a prestidigitator's trick, like a scarlet kerchief conjured out of a black top hat, Edmund Wilson in his prime would reemerge before our astonished eyes.

After his death every room in the house in Wellfleet withered: the blue room, so much Elena's, suffered from the disappearance of its important visitor, the imperious Old King Cole. In the kitchen, with a lightened workload, Elena appeared more tired, vaguer than before, and the ashtrays were filled to overflowing. The formal sitting room, Mary McCarthy's domain, looked like a funeral parlor; the dining room was as closed as a summer hotel at season's end and the stacks of books in the bedrooms looked dull with disuse. My husband and I felt ill at ease in the spaciousness of Edmund's wing: our privileged intimacy with the library was wasted and we shared the wish to flee from the deserted house.

Elena, always at home in the outdoors, led us to an unfrequented beach discovered by her and Brown on their off-season rambles. Here we were unaware of the vacationers nearby, packed like sardines on other sands accompanied by their transistors and their picnic hampers of martinis and the areas for nude bathers that had grown into a focal attraction for tourist curiosity, like a zoo or a freak show. Brown trotted briskly, with a proprietary air, at the water's edge. The harsh cries of gulls interrupted the monotonous crash of the waves, and our prone bodies were three dots punctuating the grandeur of solitude. Soothed, we sensed that the implacability of nature was an antidote to the implacability of death. Elena reveled like a dolphin in the buffeting, rolling waves. Then, saturated by salt, encrusted with sand, we made our way through the woods to a secret pond, tepid and dark green from the reflection of leaves and its mud bottom. It was an "aftercure" following the ocean's rough massage. We bathed languidly in the freshwater basin. I watched Elena surfacing: only her face emerged. With her hair slicked severely back I was astonished by her beauty: her eyes intensely blue against the tan of her skin, the cheekbones, the sensitive nose, the puckered mouth were familiar. Yet she looked different, as though I were seeing her for the first time, as strange as a dryad. "You look like Greta Garbo!" I exclaimed. She scowled. I had displeased her in some way. "Oh, all that is finished," she said. At that moment I understood that despite her sad role of widow and the mounting years, Elena was still growing. For her, experience was like a stone dropped into the depth of a pond, causing widening circles to appear on its serene surface. She was reluctant to look back and she associated her beauty with the past. She did not realize that this was a new beauty, very much part of today. But I took comfort in the thought that growing old does not of necessity mean diminishment. I watched Elena swimming with sure graceful strokes toward the far shore, surrounded by the quiet dignity of the wooded scene at the close of day.

A year has passed since our last visit to Wellfleet, but the house is firmly reestablished in recollection as though it had been materially repaired and endowed with new vigor. Even Mary McCarthy's waxwork parlor has been converted into an office for Elena, and Edmund's library, in the hands of assessors in preparation for sale, has, nevertheless, been restored in my mind's eye to its original state. At Thanksgiving time, my husband and I settled once more into the Wilson wing. We were still intruders, although we agreed with Elena that this section of the house should not be relegated to a shrine. But we felt like visitors to a famous grave. The Hebrew inscription enduring in place near Edmund's desk had lost its meaning. It had become an archaic scrawl proclaiming the futility of human effort rather than its glory.

But something new had been added to the library. On an open drop-leaf table a series of paper folders were arranged in neat rows. White and rectangular, they resembled tombstones in a well-kept cemetery. They were labeled: "1912," "The '20s," "The '30s," "The '40s," "The '50s," "The '60s" and "The '70s" — the letters of Edmund Wilson that Elena had been gathering and editing during many months in preparation for publication.

That day we did not go outside. The dunes etched sharply against the November sunshine were abandoned by us. We remained in the library reading: letters conjuring up Wilson's childhood already dedicated to a precocious passion for books, Princeton days, followed by World War I, then Greenwich Village and its vanished tribe of devotees led by the flaming Edna St. Vincent Millay, the thirties — Depression years — the rise and fall of the Soviet ideal, old friends, their deaths, joys, grief and the solace of work — literature, politics, art in review, travel, a cast of characters picked from the staff and writers of *The New Republic*, *Van-*

ity Fair, and later *The New Yorker,* World War II, Europe binding its wounds, the Joseph McCarthy era, the fifties and sixties — recently fled — already history, the seventies and Edmund's last days; his increasing prickly isolation and his love for the land where were his roots. We read on greedily, the vista spread before us like a film in which we lost ourselves. But we found Edmund Wilson more clearly outlined than when he had been living: the abrasive but generous, dedicated, honest, cranky, brilliant individualist. He loomed behind the events and the people analyzed and described in his correspondence. There he was, exploding with enthusiasm or disdain, rotund and owl-like with his claret-color, hooded eyes. The paper folders were not a graveyard. Rather they were steps toward a kind of resurrection suited to that bookish wizard, the presiding genius of the study-fortress. Edmund Wilson and his library were alive again.

We read through most of the night. And when we gathered in the kitchen at breakfast time no one was tired. We were exhilarated, a victorious army of three that had been present at the routing of death and passing time. Elena was puttering absent-mindedly between stove and table. Her worn slacks and sweater had elegance, her wavy blond hair was fairer because of the gray and she was glowing as though just off the ski slopes of an Alpine resort in the days of her youth.

The Dream

*A*t night on board the QE 2 the illumination in the gambling salons was as bright as department store Christmas lighting — or, perhaps, it was more like the merciless glare in operating rooms. The cruisers swarmed around the green baize card tables and the roulette wheels. Everyone was bejeweled, in full evening regalia, but under the strong lights faces were putty gray and weirdly aged.

The croupier, Leopold Litvak, presided, blade-thin in his impeccable tuxedo. His swarthy foreign countenance and low broad brow were topped by a plume of black curls. His inscrutable jet eyes were focused on the gamblers as though siphoning into himself their innermost secrets.

"Mesdames, Messieurs, faites vos jeux."

Roland Ostrum placed his chips with hesitation, never having played roulette before. He was president of a large mail-order corporation. Born on a farm in Iowa, he had worked his way up the business ladder and there was no room in his life for more than his mail-order concern, his wife and his children, about whom he bragged collectively and individually. He was blond and fair skinned with a wide mouth that was often stretched into a candid grin. His wife, Sally, was by his side. She was short and plump and her face had the serene beauty of a peasant

Madonna. At Radcliffe she had majored in modern dance and drama, but her family of six had reduced her ardor for the theater. Recently, she had been directing amateur groups in Morristown, New Jersey, near the Ostrum home. It had been she who had urged her husband, newly a young millionaire, to join the cruise. He had no curiosity about the world, traveling as seldom as possible and then only on business. Amusements, frivolity, all vices were foreign to him; he neither smoked nor drank but, occasionally, to keep his associates company, he would sip a little glass of sweet crème de cacao. On board the QE 2 he had been behaving strangely, as though a bland drink of milk had been spiked with strong spirits. At this moment his gambling stakes were perilously high.

"Rien ne va plus," murmured Leopold Litvak.

The wheel began to spin. Sally Ostrum felt quite giddy. She was reminded of those carousel rides with her children, when, mounted on a gaudily painted horse with the youngest held firmly in front of her on the hard wooden saddle, she had watched the riders bobbing up and down, around and around, while each in turn clutched in vain at the brass ring, always just out of reach. The kaleidoscopic shapes and colors settled into place, the merry-go-round slowed down — the roulette wheel ceased to spin. The croupier, adroitly manipulating his rake, gathered in the chips. The gamblers were unaware that in this game no one was ever winner. Leopold Litvak's face remained an impassive mask as the young millionaires divested themselves of more and more money. Sally touched her husband's sleeve. "Don't you think you have played enough?" "Leave me alone. You can go if you want to." Roland Ostrum placed his bet.

"Mesdames, Messieurs, faites vos jeux."

The wheel twirled, came to a halt. Again the chips slid toward the croupier as though magnetized. And like a magnet, Leopold Litvak's glance held the crowd in check. Aroused at *last, the young millionaires and wives were growing restive and alarmed. Yet they were unable to stop. Stakes rose, the wheel revolved faster, the air grew electric. When wallets and purses were empty, earrings, bracelets, rings, necklaces, studs, cufflinks and watches were substituted for money. The game and the players seemed to be whirling like confetti around the still, sardonic figure of the croupier.*

Abruptly, a change occurred. The scene shifted smoothly, the roulette wheel faded away, a stage appeared in its place. Leopold Litvak stood on the apron above the footlights. His black tuxedo had turned into a swallowtail, sequined like a mermaid's fin. He was wearing a baby blue top hat beneath which his swarthy face retained all its dignity and suavity. The costume was out of an old-fashioned vaudeville act, but Litvak's clipped faintly foreign accent did not belong to the conventional master of ceremonies.

"Ladies and gentlemen, which one of you will draw from my hat the lucky number?"

In another transformation the gambling area of the QE 2 was dwindling until it fitted inside the frame of a television screen. Leopold Litvak, the young millionaires, their wives emerged in lurid Technicolor. A red velvet curtain at the rear of the stage parted, revealing a display of dining room furniture in "Swedish modern," the table set with garish china and an artificial-flower centerpiece. It was not the type of home decoration to delight the spoiled millionaires, but they pressed forward avidly like a revolutionary mob about to witness an execution.

"Number seventeen has it!" Litvak held the card high. "Who is the fortunate winner? Step up! Step up!"

Pamela Mellow raised her hand shyly, a schoolgirl ready with an uncertain answer to the teacher's question. She was propelled ahead until she stood on stage, posed in front of the dining room suite, her long yellow hair falling artfully over her pretty shoulders. Across the television screen flashed the words: "Meet Miss America in her luxurious home." The picture wavered and the table and chairs vanished, replaced, in turn, by a refrigerator, a camera, a tractor, a yacht. The passengers were growing frantic: shouting, pushing, stamping. As their blind greed increased, they grabbed with equal passion at a Mercedes Benz and at an A&P display of detergents. Al Oberdorfer staggered proudly off stage clutching a giant garbage pail while the audience clapped and cheered.

Leopold Litvak no longer restrained the crowd; instead, like a galvanized ray, his black glance was evoking frenzy. He was a sorcerer among the grotesque apparitions of his own conjuring.

On a moving platform, a wax dummy swathed in sables was on exhibition. "Number thirteen! Who has number thirteen?"

Sally Ostrum shrieked and pushed forward. It looked as though she might be stampeded before reaching the stage. With mock gallantry Leopold Litvak helped her up. She clawed at the dummy tearing the coat away as though she were engaged in deadly combat. Her screams grew more strident and she jumped up and down in an obscene dance that in no way resembled the practiced movements of her Radcliffe days. The fur coat was transferred from the dummy to Sally's body, and during the exchange the lights were lowered. Wax melted into flesh, as stark naked now, the mannequin glided insouciantly into the wings, accompanied by renewed applause and the roaring of the spectators. Sally Ostrum stood alone on stage, wildly disheveled, clutching the sable coat in an attempt to cover her tattered dress and exposed underwear. She continued to jump up and down in place, shouting hoarsely, senselessly.

Below the footlights, Roland Ostrum watched his wife. The broad grin spreading over his face no longer candid, his lips were stretched in a frozen grimace of uncomprehending pain.

The picture flickered and the television screen went blank.

A PLEASURE DOME

THE "PLAYHOUSE" constructed by Otto Waldman according
to his own design was octagonal. Around its circumference
embrasured seats deeply cushioned in pink and purple (his
racing colors) were like stained glass inversely casting re-
flections upon the window-walls of the all-purpose room.
Otto Waldman seemed to form an architectural part of the
setting with his solid body, great bony nose like a jutting
buttress, deep-set dark eyes under craggy brows, and generous mouth with large, square, separated teeth suggesting
stone carving. But his charm, mobility and inquisitive rest-
lessness contradicted this monumentality. In his midfif-
ties, his only concession to age was in the thinning and
graying of his straight black hair, which he wore long to
conceal the bald patches. His wife, Edith, several years his
elder, retained the fair prettiness of her youth, only slightly
faded. But in the harsh light of the playhouse her skin
looked fragile and drained of color.

The Waldmans' country home was in Roslyn, Long Island. Since their children were grown they had sold the
big house across the road and had installed themselves in a
converted Colonial farm, a small jewel set in an English garden enclosed by tall delphiniums in every shade of blue, as

spiked as cypress trees. The Waldmans had kept their many acres of woods and fields through which Otto went horseback riding in the early morning before taking off for the city and the investment banking firm where he was a partner. But his restless nature never permitted him to settle for long. Soon after Edith had completed the decorating of the new house, Otto was directing his darting eyes higher to the top of the hill, the pinnacle of his property: it was to be the site for the octagonal playhouse.

"For our old age," he had explained.

But the garish eccentricity of this latest dwelling would have been more suitable for an annex to a sultan's palace and Edith, reclining languid and graceful against the pink and purple cushions, might have been the chief wife in the harem. The building was still incomplete, but Otto had proudly shown my husband and me all the conveniences under construction: the latest and best of everything. When finished it was to be a self-sufficient unit; the converted farm would be deserted at the bottom of the hill. Otto drove us up in his jeep, rattling and crashing all the way. But it seemed to me that it was the accelerated energy of our host rather than the rocky roadbed that was the cause for our uneasy ride.

*

We had known the Waldmans for many years, almost a generation, having met them at a PTA meeting at the "progressive" nursery school attended by our children. Monday through Friday, at 9:00 A.M. and at noon, a crowd of urchins dressed in flapping windbreakers and parkas, tattered blue jeans, sneakers with laces untied would swarm over the sidewalks in front of Number 6 East 82nd Street. Stamping, pushing, shoving, butting one another they paid no heed to the herding attempts of the maids, nurses, governesses and harassed mothers who accompanied them. The Jefferson School was founded on the formula of "freedom and informality." Inside there was a lingering musty smell, left over, perhaps, from the more dignified former life of the house. Now the rooms were furnished with Jungle gyms and other climbing apparatus, sandboxes and diminutive, gaily painted tables and chairs. Books, blackboards, all schoolroom implements, were conspicuously absent. At the Jefferson School academic learning was taboo. The parents paid heavily for the privilege of their offspring's instruction in the skills of aggression, self-defense and clambering useful to a population of Pygmies in some undiscovered Congo village.

At the meeting the mothers and fathers crouched on the dwarf chairs listening submissively to their children's guides. These, perhaps, were uniformly childless and youthful, but they were paled from the noise, violence and confusion that whirled about them each morning from nine to twelve. They possessed, however, the burning self-righteousness of missionaries. The parents, on the other hand, mainly successful members of the professional class, looked humble and apologetic. The "rod and the rule," banished during the day, cast their punitive shadows at these evening sessions. As in a courtroom, the mothers and fathers were found guilty: the ignoring of Oedipus and Electra complexes and a variety of environmental deficiencies constituted their crimes. Next to me I noticed a man, different from the others. He was leaning forward eagerly, curious rather than shame-faced. Like a vacuum cleaner switched to high voltage, he was absorbing the special jargon of the faculty. He had a massive head of Indian-straight black hair, a large sharp jutting nose, snapping eyes under prominent brows — all his features as well as his powerful body seemed to be engaged in dynamic resorbing, while around him the rest of us were dwindling under the stern judgment of our oppressors. I examined his wife also, as pliant as he was solid, fair in contrast to dark. She looked feminine and romantic, Edwardian — Irene out of Galsworthy's *Forsyte Saga*, dressed in pastel tie silk from the "young moderns" department of Lord & Taylor's or Bloomingdale's. After final instructions on the way to react to their children in the home, the parents were dismissed. My husband and I started a conversation with our neighbors and from that time began our long association with Otto and Edith Waldman.

At this period they were living in a cramped apartment on the Upper East Side. Otto had just joined a renowned banking firm, and he still held a beginner's position. In his early thirties, he had already left behind several careers: lumberjack in Canada, teacher of history in an upstate college, inventor of mechanical patents, free-lance writer. His education had been sporadic too. His brilliant, quick fitful mind moved about in many directions, but as soon as it was halted in a fixed situation Otto grew bored and he was on to something new. Now with Edith to fortify his purpose, he had settled down to making money, a preoccupation that had for him the elements of a game of chess, fascinating but not altogether serious. Their apartment consisted of two rooms; Edith had wanted a good address near Fifth Avenue. The children, son Lee and daughter Elizabeth, shared a bedroom, and after their guests had gone, Otto and Edith turned the living room into their own sleeping quarters. But everyone who knew the Waldmans realized that this home was temporary. Otto's erratic drive combined with Edith's steady determination would soon move them upward.

Edith Moffat had been born and raised in Hannibal, Missouri, her father's family having migrated there from Virginia. On the maternal side, she was descended from the early settlers of Nantucket Island. Though she lacked the cosmopolitan urbanity of Otto's German-Jewish background, she did not underrate her own early American roots, and she was resolved that her children should have the advantage of both. That included money, a great deal of it. Edith, despite her delicate appearance, was hardheaded, and she placed her faith in that extraordinary machine, Otto's brain. It was her duty to make certain that it would no longer become derailed, and to this end she extended her maternal role to include him as well as the children. At this Jefferson School age, they looked alike, two stocky wild ponies, but Edith's eyes peered from under Lee's shaggy, tawny bangs, while Elizabeth's tomboy antics suggested Otto's unbridled energy.

*

"Let's swim!" Otto was saying as he jumped up from a cushioned seat in his playhouse. Even here, in his own pagoda, he soon felt confined and must rush outside to the pool extended before him like a liquid, aquamarine magic carpet.

*

Shortly after our meeting, the Waldmans moved two blocks eastward from their cooped-up apartment to a town house on 95th Street. It was opposite the Kronenbergers' home where I had met Philip Rahv on that snowy Saint Patrick's Day night. But even today, when I find myself in that neighborhood, abandoned now by both the Kronenbergers and the Waldmans, number 133, outwardly unchanged, with the same varnished bright blue front door, seems a

continent removed from the high stoop down which Nathalie Rahv had floated with so much buoyancy and dignity
and the living room ringing with the heated arguments of
the ex-Stalinists. At the Waldmans' were to be found the
denizens of big business. Otto had become the youngest
partner at his law firm, and Edith had adapted herself with
ease and grace to their new station.

As for Lee and Elizabeth, they had been removed from
the Jefferson School. Lee now sported a blue blazer, correct
gray flannels and a visored cap with an initial, emblem of
an academy for the sons of the rich. Elizabeth wore the
uniform of an old-fashioned girls' seminary. In certain
areas of New York City the dark jumper and white shirt
were as recognizable as a nun's habit. But Elizabeth still
looked untamed, and in spite of Edith's firm bridling, the
wild streak, inherited from Otto, would remain. Our son
and the Waldman children had grown apart. He had gone
on with "progressive" education and dressed in the
required flapping parka, blue jeans and worn sneakers, a
juvenile, private-school socialist, he was separated from his
capitalistic counterparts by a gulf of mutual snobbery.

Yet my husband and I continued to be friends with the
Waldmans. A new member of the family had been added
to the house on 95th Street. Edith, an only child, had imported her aging widowed mother from Hannibal. Mrs.
Moffat would not appear at formal parties, but on more
intimate occasions she could be found in her special armchair in the snugness of the "den." She was a diminutive
spare woman who never permitted herself to recline. Her
knobby arthritic fingers were perpetually busy sewing but-
tons on her grandchildren's uniforms or knitting afghans
against the cold of a New York City winter. She wore her
hair in a severe gray topknot and there was something un-

compromising in the angles of her small person. I felt that she was silently yearning to return to the backporch gossip of her home in Hannibal and that she regarded this house as a prison and her dutiful daughter a jailer. She rarely expressed an opinion, but I would sometimes catch her looking at her son-in-law through her steel-rimmed spectacles with an expression of incredulity tinged with disapproval. To the prim penuriousness of her New England heritage, he must have appeared like a crazy Oriental potentate. Before long, Mrs. Moffat moved away to her own apartment in a nearby residential hotel. I could imagine her there companioned by a few mementos preserved from former days: Victorian rocker, a clock under a glass dome, an heirloom silver tea service and her late husband's inkwell in the shape of Missouri's capitol building. She would write letters back home, and in a refined fashion she might even boast about her son-in-law's money and her daughter's fashionable life-style, but she would remain, to the day of her death, in exile, prisoner to their wealth.

Houses crumble in memory as surely as do people. Yet the details of a room, the slope of a roof, the curve of a driveway are often easier to summon than the tilt of a chin, a certain expression or a special way of walking. In the case of Otto Waldman, the contrary is true. I see him emerging from the woods of his Long Island weekend and summer estate: he is carrying a machete and is sweating from his efforts in clearing a path, cutting away underbrush, chopping down a tree. I see his craggy face, jutting nose, prominent brows, his strong body, and in my mind's eye I supply him with an Indian's feathered headdress and the machete turns into a tomahawk. Behind him, gradually, the house, which has been lost to memory, comes into focus; it is spic and span white but the interior is dark. On every table Lowestoft bowls are filled with Edith's prize roses. I see the glass-enclosed porch, the gathering place for cocktails. It abuts on the cutting garden, the farmer's cottage, the stable, the greenhouse that nurtures orchids ranging from fleshy white and purple trumpets to sprays of chartreuse butterfly cymbidiums. Almost all of the living quarters face in this direction. A pleasant hilly vista is glimpsed only from the front upon arrival: the house is turned the wrong way. It seems to be saying something about the Waldmans' way of life: was their amassing of possessions too rapid? Did their wealth bring them as much confusion as satisfaction? At any rate, one was conscious everywhere of the odd architectural flaw.

A different group made their appearance here. Added to Otto's banking associates were his recently collected horsy friends. He had taken up hunting with the innocent gusto with which he attacked any new experience. His riding companions regarded him with wonder, a latecomer, an outsider; they marveled at his daring. "Otto really doesn't know how to ride. He has a terrible seat," they said in their slightly nasal drawls, "and yet in some ways he's better than any of us." I had a vision of our host, handsome in his hunting pink, booted and spurred. He was bouncing in the saddle and (like his house), he was faced backward toward the rear of his galloping steed! But at the end of the chase it was he who held the trophy aloft by its bushy tail, the triumph of crude nerve over effete training.

From all his homes Otto would leave on frequent flying business trips to Europe, the Far East and across the United States. Not contented to be just another partner, he had become, as well, an entrepreneur, a solo operator. Like his friends from the hunt, his business colleagues watched him with astonishment mixed, in this case, with envy. Again it was he who captured the spoils, now in the form of industrial mergers. Once, on his return from Munich, I asked him about the reconstruction of that city. "How should I know," he had answered. "I never set foot outside. I leave the plane, I'm picked up by a company limousine, chauffeured to the conference room, then straight back to the airport and the flight home." What seemed to be a far-flung journey was a kind of trap in which Otto's galvanic mind was confined to columns of figures and his keen eyes looked out on nothing but the narrow trajectory of speed.

*

"I hope you aren't famished," Edith was saying. "We are going to have a picnic. The Frigidaire isn't connected yet and the stove doesn't work." There was still a trace of Southern accent in her speech and she sounded exhausted. Perhaps this latest move had been too much for her, or it could have been the lassitude of boredom, as this time it had been Otto, not she, who had been the chief planner and decorator. The playhouse was all his and she had been reduced to a guest in her own home. Otto and my husband were already swimming; two energetic, emphatic men, their enormous splashings overcrowded the pool. It was a hazy day in early September, and although the air was warm the sun had lost its strength and its gold had turned to wan silver. I had reluctantly put summer behind me for another year and I longed for a crisp cool day, a harbinger of fall to strengthen my resolve and to disperse the melancholy of the dying season.

"Come on in, it's great," Otto urged, pausing for a moment on the ledge at the shallow end. The pool was tepid, too, but when I got out I shivered in the sultry air.

"Food, at last," Otto announced, following me out of the water.

Another jeep had arrived on the hilltop and a butler appeared carrying wicker picnic hampers and an umbrella. "I thought you might be needing this, madam."

"Thank you, Jones." In the mauve wash under the unfurled shelter Edith's skin had an indoor look. It was never exposed to the sun and only the lateness of the season and the lack of accessories for the new pool had made her venture outside unprotected.

I watched Jones spreading a pink cloth. He set out the silver, glass and china as though he were at the Ritz. His manner was discreet, obsequious yet superior, but he looked like a retired pugilist, with a drinker's red face and a squashed nose. Otto had said that he was newly imported from Ireland, another addition to the playhouse, and I was sure I had seen him somewhere before, going through the same ritual gestures. Suddenly, in one of those dreamlike transformations that memory delights in performing, the pagoda and the pool, like a revolving set, slid away and Jones was acting his part against a Palladian manor house on a terrace in Galway, Ireland.

*

It had been our first visit to Ireland, still peaceful in 1965. On arrival at Dublin, my husband and I were greeted by an unwelcoming downpour. An Irish author acquaintance was waiting at the airport to take us for a drive through the city. I strained eagerly to see out of the blinded windows of the car, but the little I could discern looked dingy, disappointing, faintly familiar, and our tour was an exclusively literary one, taking us from one James Joyce shrine to the next. Even the famous Georgian houses were a disenchantment, neglected and lifeless tenements that had seen better days, as was Trinity College, a gray stone quadrangle enclosing a plot of bright green grass: the continent of Aca-

tual hostages. During his leisure he even wrote a book about his collection, published with handsome illustrations in full color. But his leisure was decreasing, his flying trips growing more and more frenetic until it was a question of who was master, he or the jet, that powerful time- and space-consuming monster.

The Waldmans' friends were often received by Edith alone. She no longer suggested the romantic Irene out of *The Forsyte Saga* but a matron from the boom period before the thirties' stock market crash. She would be wearing a low-cut evening gown that displayed to advantage her smooth, delicately boned white naked back and jewels grown larger and more lustrous with the years. It pleased her to dress in the purple and pink of Otto's racing colors. Her femininity and prettiness persisted, but as the level-headed custodian of so many possessions she had developed the manner and weary poise of those closely connected with affairs of state.

"Otto will join us presently," she would say. "He just flew in from Cairo and he leaves tomorrow for Dallas at the crack of dawn. It's not realistic — " This last was stated without conviction. Otto's moneymaking propensities were, indeed, very real to her, a necessity, as this new home proved.

Although reduced in number the rooms were large, with a lofty view across Central Park that looked like an extension of the apartment itself. At night the lights in the skyscrapers and even the stars seemed to belong to the Waldmans — another collection displayed against black velvet instead of white silk. Masses of orchids from the Long Island greenhouse were everywhere. In her decorating Edith had been attracted by jewel tones: emerald in the foyer; the spacious paneled library, ruby; the drawing

deme, the same the world over. For a passing hour at lunch at a writers' club I felt that I was actually in the Ireland of Molly Bloom and the Dubliners. The room was bare and drafty, but around the table the fluent gab was warm, excluding the streaming rain outside and adding spice to the bland white fish on our plates. Afterward our guide insisted on resuming the tour, driving us to the tower of Stephen Dedalus and additional Joyce monuments. At last we succeeded in shaking him and proceeded by ourselves to Galway to the Waldmans', the goal of our visit.

Otto, having learned all there was to know about hunting on Long Island, lost interest in it. On one of his trips to London he had made a detour to Ireland and, impulsively, had bought a house in the horse country of Galway. Once again Edith was called upon to furnish a new home, this time out of the antique stores of London. She did this with enthusiasm, but when she was finished the house became her prison. She did not ride and she was surrounded by people who apparently did little else. One winter's day I met her at a New York City restaurant after her return from a stay in Galway. She was looking especially beautiful, her face latticed by a black veil pinned to a fur beret. "Good heavens," she exclaimed, shrugging out of her mink coat, "I am so happy to be back. You can't imagine what it is like there at this time of year! Mud and more mud and all those heavy dirty boots lying in the foyer. And now Otto is talking about moving to Ireland permanently. Of course I won't hear of it. He can't leave the firm now, just when Lee and Elizabeth are about ready for college. It's not realistic," she added, a favorite phrase of hers. Edith in her pliant fashion, always the strong one, would prevail and Galway was to remain just another vacation spot.

A few years later, just before our visit in late June, Otto,

miraculously, had been made co-whip of the Galway Blazers, along with a famous moving picture director of Irish ex-
traction. It was evening when my husband and I finally arrived, and although the rain had let up it was too dark to
see the place. The Waldmans were on the threshold of their
neoclassical doorway. Inside, the rooms were kin to those I
had known on East 95th Street and Roslyn. Again I felt the
disappointment of the traveler in quest of the exotic who
discovers that alien roads may extend in directions similar
to those he has left behind at home. Here were Edith's
roses in Lowestoft bowls and the recognized imprint of her
taste on the furnishings.

But the guests were new: Anglo-Irish, their language, though supposedly mine, sounded like a foreign
tongue and the subject of their conversation was exclusively
equine: the care, breeding and conformation of horses; the
land, its condition and suitability for hunting; the weather
during last season's hunt and predictions for next. They
were all in evening dress but they looked shabby beside the
resplendence of the host and hostess. While her company
displayed the calm of impenetrable self-confidence, Edith
appeared uncertain. Otto was scrutinizing his guests with
that expression I had first noted at the PTA meeting at the
Jefferson School. The vacuum cleaner was again switched
to high voltage, but instead of Freudian terminology he was
now resorbing the chatter peculiar to these Irish lovers of
horses. He was quite aware of his differences, an urban
nouveau riche in the midst of the land-poor gentry. He
knew that it was his American dollars that opened the port-
cullis to him, but he crossed the moat in high good spirits
and without pretentions.

Early the next morning I went outside for my first look at
the property. Now there was no disappointment. From

the terrace field after field, sectioned by low stone walls,
stretched away to the horizon. Here and there shallow
milky ponds were like fallen clouds. The mercurial sky
changing from rosy to blue to gray, emphasized the tran-
quility of the land. A few horses were grazing quietly in
the rough dewy grass. Their silhouettes suggested the full
hunt of which they would be part, just as in an artist's
sketch a portrait drawn in impressionistic lines will later be
incorporated into the richness of an oil painting. Surveying
the same scene, his back toward me, I espied Otto. He had
one foot firmly planted on a wall and, for once, he too was
still. The pose of this isolated figure was conspicuous, even
aggressive against the wide placid landscape. He was the
conqueror, the acquirer accepted but never assimilated into
the ranks of the conquered.

Otto's collection of antique snuffboxes glittered like
crown jewels in cabinets lined in white watered silk. The
Waldmans had moved from the house on East 95th Street to
an apartment on Fifth Avenue, after Lee and Elizabeth had
departed for their respective boarding schools and Edith
had grown tired of housekeeping complications in her numerous scattered homes. "It's not realistic," she would say.
Yet there was nothing simple about this new abode situated
around the corner from that first apartment from which it
was removed not only by ten years of time but by the accre-
tion of many opulent objects in space. Geographically, the
Waldmans had come full circle, but in their mode of living
they were still spiraling upward. The snuffboxes wer
symbols: gold, silver, enameled, filigreed, bejeweled, the
were once the property of kings, queens, courtiers a
courtesans, but now Otto had taken possession of them
had locked them inside their white moiré cages. He w
examine their miniature elegance as though they wer

room, amethyst and turquoise; the dining room, crystal and pearl.

In all this there was one discordant note: over the marble mantel in the living room hung the painting by Francis Bradford of the bewitched man-child-dwarf-sprite seated in the field of tiger lilies beneath a primitive moon. My husband and I had introduced the Waldmans to the Bradfords, and Otto, always intrigued by any world not yet his own, had carried off this painting. It is certain that he paid a handsome price for it. Transplanted from the Connecticut barn it continued its existence on alien territory, face to face with a gilded ancient Chinese screen. The awed flutist, intent on his night sky, was ignorant of the formal intricate secrets of the East, though separated from them in the Waldmans' living room only by the luxurious divide of an Aubusson carpet. I alternately studied and looked away from the painting. It was an oasis, as though the familiar roar of traffic should give way to a hush more obtrusive than noise and, in a mysterious fashion, more threatening. The manikin in the painting had become an oracle, mute instead of blind. Silent flute in hand, he seemed to be issuing a warning to all of us assembled, guests and hosts alike, but we were not empowered to hear it.

*

At the playhouse on Long Island we were enjoying the picnic: champagne (Edith's sole alcoholic beverage), caviar and smoked salmon sandwiches, hearts of artichoke and late raspberries from the garden.

Otto's mood was expansive; his dark eyes danced but his body was like a coiled spring. "How do you like it?" he asked again and again. "This is where Edith and I are going to play — no worries, no responsibilities. We are going to turn our old age into youth. Oh, it's going to be perfect!" he said.

"If it ever gets finished," added Edith.

The pagoda was never completed. Soon after that warm September afternoon Edith, with shocking suddenness, without warning, was felled by a paralytic stroke. After many months in the hospital she returned to the apartment and I was allowed to visit her. She received me in a wheel-chair, attended by a nurse, a lady-in-waiting to the distorted image of Edith. One useless leg in a heavy iron brace, one lifeless arm cradled in a pink and purple flowered silk scarf were the badges of her martyrdom. Her speech was strange and thick, sometimes rational, sometimes not. Occasionally, words out of context issued from her mouth, delivered as it were, by someone else, an invisible presence speaking through her — indifferent, alike, to her confusion and the painful effort of her discourse. "It's like pressing the wrong key on a typewriter," she apologized. "It just happens."

Despite her affliction, she looked unnaturally youthful. All the lines in her face had been smoothed away, leaving her skin like white, pink-tinted porcelain. Her hair had grown to shoulder length during her stay in the hospital, and now it was brushed and combed to silk by the medical lady-in-waiting. The managing woman who, for all those years, had stood behind Otto had vanished. In her place was a broken doll bearing her name.

The Waldmans moved to England. I have not seen them again. Elizabeth married one of the sons of the Galway gentry. I picture her fox hunting as though to the manor born, jumping the low stone walls with an ease that had never been granted her father. But she will not stop here. Lee works at the London Exchange, and I see him wearing bowler and chamois vest. On the streets he is indistinguishable from the other toilers in the City.

Otto has entered a new phase and he no longer sees his former friends and associates. I have heard that the Waldmans' home forms part of a graceful crescent overlooking a leafy London square. But the house is equipped with a complicated system of ramps and escalators designed by Otto. Edith is still immobile; she still wears brace and sling and is attended by nurses. Those strange words continue to fall like marbles from her pink, perfectly painted lips. Otto revolves around her, but she is as unresponsive, now, as an idol.

Like the fisherman and his wife of the fairy tale Otto and Edith Waldman rose step by step, unaware that they were moving toward downfall, until in building his octagonal playhouse for their old age, Otto attempted to defy time itself. With that, his plans crashed about him, Edith was sacrificed and the pleasure dome remained a dream, forever out of reach.

The Dream

*T*here was to be a shipboard wedding. For one night it would take the place of the other entertainments offered to the Young Millionaires' Club on the QE 2: the bingo games, the films, nostalgic blues singers and all the rest of the variety acts. It was to be a splendid affair — true, the participants had been living together for five years and were enjoying connecting staterooms on this cruise. Yet the bride-to-be was planning a spectacle in keeping with her philosophy of life and commerce. Donna Starr (originally Doris Stein) was president of a cosmetics firm and she used her person as its trademark. On the fringe of New York's jet set, her photograph was familiar in the newspapers: attending openings, modeling new fashions, advertising her own products. Because of this she chose her accessories with utmost care, believing in the efficacy of both repetition and change to build the privileged image of "chic." She was never without her oversized rose-tinted spectacles, although her eyes were perfection: twenty-twenty vision, large and clear, each false lash applied with loving expertise to compose a setting for two flawless topaz stones. Her hair matched her eyes, straightened by a renowned hairdresser, it fell artlessly on either side of her face like a parted golden curtain softening the contours of her square jaw. Her clothes were cas-

ual, expensive, innovative — as were all her belongings. On this voyage an old-fashioned steamer trunk, discovered in a junk shop, graced her cabin. It might once have been the property of a Russian princess, starting its career aboard a luxury turn-of-the-century wagon-lit bound from Saint Petersburg to the Riviera companioned by a shining samovar. Long ago it had weathered its first Atlantic crossing; hooked to a baseboard it creaked and groaned in time to the liner's rise and fall, washed by salt breezes from an open porthole. On board the QE 2 it stood free — there were no lurchings nor any smell of the sea. With age the steamer trunk had lost its air of adventure. Inside Donna Starr's stateroom it had deteriorated into just an "amusing" piece of furniture, with obsolete brass locks and corners, quaint drawers and hanging space still haunted by the smell of patchouli left over from the long-deceased Russian princess.

The morning of the wedding found Donna Starr and Adrian Mendez-Cohen, her groom-to-be, sharing her triple-width bed. Adrian was president of a brokerage house, but he found plenty of time to maintain himself in impeccable trim. Outside the covers, a bare arm and shoulder were firm and tan — he and Donna had recently visited his tropical hideaway near Trinidad. In sleep, his head had a somber Spanish beauty: a fine aquiline nose, arching dark brows, a smooth olive-complexioned oval face. Even in bed the outline of his body showed tall and athletic. Like George Eliot's fictional hero Daniel Deronda, Adrian Mendez-Cohen looked too ideal to be real. But when he opened his eyes about noon, resuming his shipboard routine that started with a before-brunch dry martini, his matter-of-fact pragmatic personality dimmed his romantic appearance as surely as the night is put to rout by the day.

At 6:00 A.M. the foghorn of the QE 2 emitted its ugly blast. The frog croaked and woke the nuptial pair. "Damn," said Donna as she read the unheard-of hour on the face of her al-

ligator-skin travel clock. She sat up, immediately putting on her outrageous pink-tinted goggles as a virgin might veil her naked breasts.

The evil noise did not abate. "We must be running into fog," Adrian said. But since the portholes were sealed fast and shrouded, no one could be certain. The croakings were blood-chilling, portentous. There had been a time when the foghorn had been a reassurance to voyagers that their captain was at his post, neither sleeping nor playing and that, in spite of unfavor-able weather, he would steer them to safe harbor.

Any novelty was welcome on board the QE 2 and now the staff collaborated to make this wedding tremendous: the chef erected a skyscraper cake decorated with spun sugar petals, a tribute to Donna Starr's cosmetic line, White Camelia. In the dining room there was a sculpture carved out of special non-melting ice; glowing by indirect lights, it read in six-foot-high letters: "Adrian and Donna." The Christmas tinsel was taken down, and artificial flowers clustered in snowy bunches like sprouts around the crystal stalks of the chandeliers. The main lounge was being turned into a chapel. Above the grand stair-case the solemn columnar pipes of an organ replaced the mosaic of the Four Winds and a map of the British Isles. All day, musicians could be heard tuning their instruments for the danc-ing.

Before the event the bridal couple circulated among the young millionaires and their wives as though this were an ordinary af-ternoon. But Donna Starr's harmonizing pale apricot make-up and Adrian Mendez-Cohen's white cashmere turtleneck and his sleek Ultrasuede white jeans constituted for the others a quasi dress rehearsal.

The Oberdorfers and the Mellows were especially thrilled. In the cocktail lounge they craned their necks for a better view of the bride and groom, who resembled a color photograph of *themselves in the "there is this to talk about" section of a slick fashion magazine. Pamela and Jill reminisced about their own weddings, recalling their gowns and those of the bridesmaids, while the men earnestly estimated, in retrospect, the wedding expenses defrayed by the families of their loved ones.*

When the hour arrived, at last, everyone trooped into the main lounge, transformed, with a red-carpeted aisle vaulted by plywood Gothic arches and a nave richly illuminated by stained glass. If closely examined, these windows revealed the image of a monster toad attended by a reptilian family of snakes, lizards, alligators and a variety of gargoyle birds with avian heads and human bodies in robes of intense purple and red. But nobody noticed. All were stirred by the sound of the organ. The familiar music brought back other days, and the eyes of the young millionaires and their wives filled with furtive self-indulgent tears and their throats were mildly constricted as they awaited the climax. Only George Gruntle appeared to be unconcerned. He sat in the last row in a wheelchair. Although he had tried on several occasions to contact the ship's doctor he had never succeeded in reaching him again and his leg brace had not been returned. Now, oblivious to the happenings around him, he was intent on cutting his fingernails.

The rear doors opened, admitting a procession of bridesmaids in conventional pastel organdy. Beneath picture hats, identical doll faces were painted exclusively in White Camelia shades. From where had they materialized? Until now, the Young Millionaires' Club had not included this complement of single girls. Again, no one questioned or seemed to notice — nor was anyone amazed at the bridesmaids' bouquets. Instead of flowers, each attendant carried a featureless wax head topped by an elaborate wig in a variety of styles: a flowing platinum fall, a nest of cherubic curls, a black pageboy coif with bangs, a golden gamine feather cut. Bouffant, sleek, long, short, they passed in review, as the passionless Salomes moved down the aisle, feminine John the Baptist heads cradled in their arms.

The bride was approaching: a shimmer of white satin, a mist of tulle. Donna Starr was concealed by yards of costly tissue. Her features hidden by a face veil with only a glint of golden hair showing through, she was as shrouded as the portholes of the QE 2. Unescorted, she walked toward the altar, where the groom was waiting for her. The bridesmaids were ranged on either side, their pretty vapid faces doubled by the featureless dummies in their gorgeous wigs.

The place behind the altar was vacant. Where was the captain who was to marry the pair? After so many preparations, would the ceremony have to be postponed? But just as the bride reached her destination, a scarlet-clad figure emerged. There was a sigh of relief, the show would go on. The cardinallike apparition tantalized the young millionaires with its familiarity, yet they were sure they had not encountered it before. He stood behind the altar so lightly poised that his august title might have been borrowed from the bird, his presence merely its representation. Glossy black hair sprang from his low broad brow, showing like plumage beneath the crimson cap. He had a beak nose and a cruel, thin-lipped mouth. His blazing eyes seemed to have an independent existence of their own, their brilliance raying beyond his face as though some power had jerked them free from their deep, wide-set sockets. He officiated in a voice so inaudible that only when the bride's veil was lifted and she merged for an instant with the groom in the customary kiss did the guests realize that the ceremony was terminated. At that instant, the cardinal reached into the voluminous folds of his skirt and drew out a small camera. The young millionaires recognized, at once, the expensive German make, the same that formed part of their own luggage. Quickly, skillfully, the prelate snapped a picture of the embracing couple, while an electric current zigzagged like lightning through the lounge. Then the recessional march struck up and the bride and groom turned to confront the crowd. Everyone gasped, for although her smooth fall of hair was still bright gold it warred, now, with her features grotesquely distorted by age. Her cheeks were furrowed in wrinkles, deep as gulches; her eyes, unshielded by her rosy glasses, had shrunk to mean slits — they and the dark gash of her lips were rents in the ravaged territory of her face. He was barely recognizable: like wax, his firm flesh had melted into flabbiness; his aquiline Hispanic beauty was engulfed by pendulous folds and lumps of fat. Unconscious of what had befallen them, the bridal pair walked triumphantly toward the exit. The scene was halted here for a moment before exploding as silently as a bubble.

SOME VIEWS OF OLD HOUSES:
VENICE AND PARIS

THE PLANE deposited us in the dark on the mainland of Venice. Within a few seconds my husband and I found ourselves alone on the pier in total stillness, nothing to be seen but the Adriatic unillumined by stars or moon. Our fellow passengers had dispersed, some with the continuing plane, others, it seemed, absorbed into the night itself. In a trickle of electricity issuing from the arrival depot, a figure approached us.

Bowing deferentially, he said, "*Signor, Signorina,* I fear you have missed the last *vaporetto* for Venice. You see, the regular season has not yet started."

Stranded, helpless, we were able to understand just enough of the flow of Italian to realize our predicament. "What are we going to do?" My question sounded like a wail.

"Do not despair, *Signorina,* I have a cousin who operates a private *vaporetto* service. I will call him at once, he will come to get you."

I tried to distinguish our rescuer in the obscurity, but all I could see was a theatrical mustache and gesticulating hands. He returned to the depot while we remained on the wharf with our valises that were like overweight, inert, mute relatives who depended on our efficiency to transport them safely from hotel to hotel. The water in front of us was unruffled by any activity. Once we caught sight of headlights moving in our direction, but they swerved and disappeared into the blackness. I felt as though a lifetime had been spent waiting. The anticipation of my first view of Venice paled. London, where, incredibly, we had lunched that noon, had receded into a memory out of youth, while home, New York City, was only a lingering intimation of some former incarnation.

A flare emerged in space, grew brighter; the purr of a motor became steadily louder and a yacht drew up to the dock. The captain, Poseidon himself, jumped out. He and his cousin engaged in a torrent of excited dialogue, incomprehensible to us, but the words *"Americano," "ricco," "Hotel Gritti Palace"* recurred at intervals. After elaborate farewells and much hand kissing we embarked. In a vessel magnificent enough for Cleopatra and her retinue, we sped, at last, toward Venice. Yet it looked as though the darkness would never be interrupted. We climbed out of the luxurious mahogany, brass-fitted cabin into the open, and I exulted in the cool air that had also embraced the walls of Venice. At last a distant constellation showed on the horizon. Slowly, silently, out of infinite space, a mirage arose, a brilliant iridescent bubble floating on the water. We had arrived. We stopped before the Gritti Palace, and Poseidon roped his boat to a post and offered me his arm. I was there and it was surprising that the ground I stood upon upheld me, that the vision I had seen was made of solid matter. My husband had the privilege of transferring a wad of bills into an open hand, then, weighted with his mortal booty, the sea god returned to his hidden realms.

The lobby of the Gritti Palace Hotel is discreetly sumptuous. Despite the lateness of the hour the concierge was impeccable in formal dress. The reception desk on which he leaned lightly might have been a balustrade and the mailboxes behind him the paneled door of a loge. He took our passports from us with the flourish of a dandy accepting a pair of proffered opera glasses, inquired solicitously about our trip and lamented the late hour of our arrival. When we related our difficulties he exclaimed, "You have been robbed! The taxi *vaporettos* leave every half-hour from the mainland to Piazza San Marco — Brigands!"

We mounted in the lift escorted by a smooth-faced bellboy in princely attire, a Cherubino carrying an oversized gold key made to unlock the trysting chamber of a Count Almaviva. I felt obscurely shamed, awkward, innocent — branded a rich American, as unconscious of the wiles of the Old World as our heavy luggage pasted with the colorful stickers of many lands.

We found our bedroom faintly royal also; the hotel had been converted from an old castle. But the blinds were closed, shutting out the Grand Canal and we could not wait until morning to explore the city. We wandered by the watery streets beneath the walls of tall palaces. Moorish windows looked down on us and statues appeared to come alive in the night. They bore witness to our progress across covered stone bridges, down narrow *calli,* hushed but for the lapping wavelets from the lagoon. We entered one piazza after another, each a separate drawing room in demilight, or a stage set furnished in Oriental and Baroque splendor. The unreality of the moment was intensified by all those ancient, inanimate, watchful objects. And in the shadows I sensed the presence of human phantoms, a company of dominoes, masks and tricornered hats swirling around us, exaggerating the sound of our solitary, solid, commonplace footfalls.

I awoke the next morning to patterns of light wheeling

across the embossed ceiling. Confused, I watched them forming and dissolving without knowing where I was. When Venice returned to me I realized that the designs were projected, like a magic lantern, by full daylight upon moving water, intercepted by the slats of shutters. Jumping out of bed I threw them wide open, and, leaning on the windowsill, I was greeted, like generations of travelers before me, by the sight of the Grand Canal. It was bordered on both sides by mansions with noble marble stairs descending into the water and tile roofs stretching into the sky. Here and there they were overtopped by cupolas and the gleam of golden crosses and angels.

On the final day of our visit my husband and I sat for the last time on the terrace of the Gritti Palace. The weather continued to be perfection, cool March sunshine, the air pure and lively; the dampness, the smell of rot that I had expected had been routed by cleansing sea breezes. By this time the vista of the Grand Canal had become familiar and I was trying to memorize it in order to take it home with me like a souvenir from a shop along the Rialto. The palaces in the sun were a lavish departure festival and the churches looked no less worldly. In my mind's eye I could now add to all this the ornate vastness of Saint Mark's Square. There, American, German, Japanese, English, French, Dutch, Scandinavian tourists are dwarfed by its immensity, their stature no more significant than the pigeons congregated over the mosaic parterre as wide as a sea. I have a photograph of my mother as a girl in the center of the piazza, kneeling to feed the birds. She is wearing a white shirtwaist, long skirt and straw boater, and the pigeons swarming around her seem to sense her gentleness. Under the arches at Florian's Café, a picture of my grandfather has been preserved, his stern profile silhouetted against the foreign newspaper he is reading. On the terrace of the Gritti Palace, as though the present riches were not enough, I also recalled the sight of Saint Mark's Church, the campanile, the Doge's Palace, the Bridge of Sighs that connects it to the dungeon across the lagoon. Just as the first settlers of Venice had built on insecure swampland, I attempted to establish the many-faceted jewel I had seen on the shifting terrain of memory — even as I realized that the vision must fade more quickly than the palaces of Venice would crumble, decay and eventually submit to the sea out of which they had arisen.

An architectural flaw is outstanding in an ideal city landscape, but it may be an enhancement just as a cast in an eye, a mole on a cheek can set off the face of a lovely woman. The *palazzo* of Peggy Guggenheim is such a defect. A latecomer, it was constructed during the nineteenth century and never completed. It consists of only two stories; its low, long, white shape resembles a houseboat moored adjacent to the darting *vaporettos* and the romantic black gondolas on the Grand Canal.

Peggy Guggenheim is one of the heirs to a copper mining fortune. She is my husband's cousin and on the night of our arrival the obsequious concierge had handed us, along with our room key, a telephone message from her. The following day we made the crossing in a gondola to visit her on the opposite bank. Through the years her house and her collection of paintings have become legendary — people beg for letters of introduction. She has been a resident of Venice since the end of the Second World War, and although I had met her in New York I was curious to see her in the foreign setting of her chosen country. Upon disembarking after our abbreviated voyage we followed a street with the name "Via Peggy Guggenheim." Part of the impregnable island had, after all, been claimed by an outsider; where the Franks had failed an American had succeeded. We approached the *palazzo* in which Peggy Guggenheim lived alone with her servants through a lush garden enclosed by high conventlike walls. I felt as though we were about to be granted an audience with the Doge.

Instead, she received us in her cool white sitting room adorned with a few modern objets d'art from her collection. Since I had last seen her, in deference to her seventy-odd years, her hair had turned white. But she was wearing a leather miniskirt, high boots and a shirt with an audaciously plunging neckline. The costume called for whips and a motorcycle. Her face was as I remembered it: the large outrageous features of a clown, her expression shrewd, candid, humorous, corrupted, yet somehow innocent. After greeting us, she asked abruptly, "How much did you give the gondolier? That's ridiculous, you overtipped him. You have to be careful, they are all thieves."

We lunched at a restaurant with tables set out on a terrace, trellised in blooming vines. Afterward Peggy argued with the waiter over the remnant of some vin ordinaire left in the carafe. In her fluent but American-accented Italian she finally bullied him into deducting it from the bill. We took a *vaporetto* bus back to her house. Standing, despite a lame leg, holding on to the pole for support, she said, "Cheaper and better than a taxi." I noticed that she was regarding the young driver, an Apollo of the people, with open admiration.

Back in her living room the shutters had been closed to the brilliant afternoon sun. Bars of light and shade striped the white walls — the convent motif again. But there was nothing nunlike about Peggy sitting with her skirt well above her knees, surrounded by her pet Chihuahuas clustering like a pack of rats about her booted legs. She and my husband exchanged family gossip and at times I caught her regarding him with the same expression she had bestowed upon the bus driver. She talked about her loneliness. "Venice is changing. It's dead. I hardly ever leave my house these days." But I wondered if it were not her life that had altered with the passing years. And I marveled that in spite of such a long expatriation she had remained so stubbornly American. She discussed her paintings, the Solomon Guggenheim Museum in New York, the rising market in art, then as a mark of favor she said, "Visiting hours will begin in a few minutes, why don't you come back this evening and see the collection by yourselves." But we preferred now. So Peggy bade us goodby, embracing my husband with appetite and, followed by her court of yapping rodents, she retired to her bedroom, explaining, "I always lock myself up when the crowd arrives."

As we moved through the gallery we might have been back in New York City at the Museum of Modern Art. It was puzzling that in the city of Titian, Tintoretto, and Tiepolo, expanses of canvas covered by Jackson Pollack's mazes of tracks could attract so many people, mostly Italians, shuffling through Peggy Guggenheim's truncated *palazzo*, as impressed and awed as though they were viewing for the first time the glories of the Church of Santa Maria della Salute. Perhaps the explanation can be found in the fact that the proud Republic having vanished forever, its flourishing commerce now ancient history, the city of Venice, picked as clean as a hollow conch shell of its moneyed aristocracy, is grateful for the presence, planted in its midst, of a representative of the wealth and culture of a new nation.

*

Peggy Guggenheim and her adopted home are linked by their shows of bravura: the island, in decline, still beautiful — she, still gallant in loneliness. And, in recall, Venice appears behind a scrim with two enlarged images: a cellar where the black water creeps up as in a well and an unfinished white *palazzo* enclosing an aging woman, the last of a line of buccaneers.

*

In Paris, in front of the Café Quai Voltaire the city is bisected by the Seine, animated by the passage of tugs, barges and sightseeing boats. There is saluting from deck to deck and up to the bridges: the Pont Neuf, the Pont Royal and the Pont du Carrousel, where the patient fishermen are forever dangling their lines in the murky water. It is an afternoon in early spring, the sky is soft monotone pale gray and the grass plots in the Tuileries Gardens are tentative green suggestions among the marble statues. Paris has always filled me with nostalgia for its history — and with the passing of time — my own.

Neighbor to the Café Quai Voltaire is the Hotel Quai Voltaire, a modest nondescript building with uniform wood shutters and iron filigree balconies, distinguished only because Oscar Wilde stayed there. Ahead, still reigning over the Gardens, is that grandiose pile of masonry: the Louvre, former palace and prison for royalty. Now the vast picture galleries are echo chambers for their ghosts. Here, beneath vaulted ceilings, the eras have jostled one another like travelers inside a palatial railroad terminal. The outside of the Louvre is being cleaned; one wing emerges ivory white while the rest is still steeped in the sooty black of age. I prefer it that way — in my memories the stones of Paris are tenebrous.

On the opposite bank, the arcades of the rue de Rivoli have also been whitened. But under them I can see a child, myself, starting out on a morning's walk with her father. He is small, compact, dapper and is wearing a newly purchased Charvet tie. He brandishes a shiny cane as he points out the sites of historical interest. My father is at ease in the Napoleonic architectural elegance of the Right Bank, but I am awed by the foreign city. I do not realize that in the years to come, bits and pieces of my own past, like particles of dust, will become imbedded in the columns, pavements, shop windows and doors of the rue de Rivoli. After strenuous sightseeing, I would visit Rumpelmayer's with my mother, where I was restored by the cold sweetness of an ice cockaded by a *qaufrette* shaped like a fan.

The rear entrance of the Hotel St. James and Albany is open on the rue de Rivoli. For many years my husband and I stayed there; it has afforded a kind of homecoming for us. From the back door one passes through a first court leading into a second, both boxed by thick ancient walls. The yards are sparingly adorned with small fountains and urns holding a few geraniums. The hotel, once the residence of the family of Madame Lafayette, later became the English Embassy, then the slightly shabby place we know. The front entrance is on the rue du Faubourg-St.-Honoré at the end of a cobbled court for car parking. The lobby is the remains of a reception hall still redolent of the past. Only a disgruntled concierge who grudgingly hands over the keys and haggles about the price of postage stamps is a reminder of the downfall of the stately mansion. We always occupy the same suite on the first floor, reached by a broad shallow flight of stairs. We can disdain the lift, which is habitually out of order. Just off the plane, "our rooms" give us welcome before we go out for a ritual midnight supper at the Régence, down the street. This restaurant is located near the Comédie Française and the Palais-Royal. It was once the meeting place for Bel Epoque after theater galas and it had withstood the tremors of the Revolutionary mobs. We return to the hotel, and for what is left of the small hours, our quarters receive us: at opposite sides of the large chamber are two brass beds equipped with an assortment of lumpy bolsters and eiderdowns; there is an old-fashioned creaky armoire, a tall wooden clothes tree as ungainly as a denuded scarecrow, as well as a collection of dilapidated armchairs upholstered in dusty red plush, diapered by demure white lace antimacassars. Everywhere the walls are hung with toile, repeating a French pastoral scene. The bathroom is cavernous, opening on to a black shaft, and the old plumbing groans regretfully. A connecting room has space for barely more than a double-size bed. This plethora of beds gives the place a rakish aspect and the mattresses seem to have retained an erotic impress of the past. All the windows face the second court. In the morning I wake to the country sounds of footsteps crunching over gravel and to bird songs — the city noises on the rue de Rivoli and the rue du Faubourg-St.-Honoré having been shut out by the thick walls. Occasionally, as though rising from a well, I hear voices. They have the special timbre belonging to French speech, not to be imitated by foreigners. But from that double bed, even the footfalls and the birds have a French cadence. Now the St. James and Albany is closed for repair, which means that our familiar rooms are being reduced to modern space-conserving dimensions. We have said a final goodby to the lumpy brass beds, the clothes tree, the armoire, and we are lodged in another hotel on the Left Bank. It has already been "repaired" and our cell-like room has nightmarish contours with corners amputated and dislocated. The bathroom is thoughtfully provided with a well-stocked bar and the elevator operates to the wheezing accompaniment of canned rock music.

Up the river from the Café Quai Voltaire I see the twin towers of Notre Dame. The view is too distant for me to discern the encrustations of carvings that cover its exterior. But I know they are there, the work of countless hands through the years attesting to the endurance of stone. The Cathedral, too, is being restored; a scaffold looks as frail as a spider's web against its mighty sides.

As far as the eye can see the bridges are hyphens joining the eighteenth- and nineteenth-century opulence of the Right Bank to the narrow medieval streets on the Left Bank. I try to absorb the mute wisdom of old houses that have outlasted so much living in the hope that they will yield their secrets of survival.

Across the avenue the book and postcard vendors are at their places. The wooden stands are like weathered shacks. In front of the café the chairs and tables appear to have been there forever, the carafes of wine, the pots of bitter coffee. Across the white cloth I once held hands, fingers locked like miniature thighs in tangled embrace. The rest is hazy; only those hands, like sculptured flesh, remain in memory. The aproned waiter seems imperishable, the fat cashier, the pedestrians: worn women dressed in mourning, carrying long loaves of bread, the bicyclists, the boulevardiers, the young lovers. A stranger saunters slowly, arrogantly by my table. He stands out from the crowd, blade-thin, swarthy, with a hawk's profile. He wears a checked cap, a sack is slung over his shoulder; he looks ageless, exiled, the perpetual wanderer. I have never seen him before yet he is familiar, a déja vu from a former existence. For an instant his penetrating, wide-set black eyes meet mine. Like a fusillade of grapeshot his glance disperses my nostalgic thoughts. Houses, all possessions are only abandoned toys, hardly more lasting than those who cling to them in vain. Nothing remains but the illusion of an arrested moment in the continuous movement of time — and the Riddle, ignored by most, pondered by a few but shared by all —

Across the Seine the soft gray sky over the shadowy hulks of the government buildings has been torn to reveal a patch of brilliant sulphurous yellow light.

The Dream

ARRIVAL

*T*he QE 2 reached its destination at the end of a week; night, and the sky was ablaze, the light as strained as an unblinking eye.   The scene teased memory like a replica from some half-forgotten recurrent dream.   Casablanca loomed over the beach: mastodon luxury hotels and condominiums exhibiting signs as large as ordinary buildings proclaiming their names in sky blue, sea green plastic sculptures that vied with one another in inventive ornamentation.   The Eden Roc, Fontainebleau, El Dorado, Rooney Plaza, Crystal Palace rose and extended in vertical and horizontal miles of concrete with thousands of balconies suspended like tubs confronting the ocean in close phalanx.   In the shallow water of the bay a flotilla of yachts was tethered, nose to nose, to the pier.   They, too, were white and, as in the hotel lobbies, one could glimpse in their cabins the forms of captive Christmas trees strung with colored bulbs winking on and off like the marquees and advertisements along Broadway.

Farther out, the United States Sixth Fleet lay at anchor in the Mediterranean.   For the entertainment of the young millionaires there was to be, on this night, a military display.

Everyone, Newmans, Mellows, Oberdorfers, Johnsons, George Gruntle, Bakers, Ostrums, Adrian Mendez-Cohen,

Donna Starr and others, trooped to the top of the QE 2, *where the squat, black, misshapen funnels reigned. On their way the voyagers passed through the ship's salons, disturbingly altered yet, like the African city, they had been seen before — where, when? At intervals the television monitors flashed the changing changeless image of Miss Rheingold in a variety of settings, always smiling her white-toothed smile. The Howard Johnson dining hall had given way to an oval Adam room, pearl gray like the inside of an oyster. Where there had been a table appointed in English china, silver and etched crystal, there now was a cage occupied by two baboons picking at each other while eating bananas, throwing the peels through the bars of their jail. "Where on earth did they come from?" Nancy Johnson asked, dilating her disdainful Zelda Fitzgerald nostrils. The organ above the grand staircase had disappeared, replaced by a full-length portrait of a beautiful woman in a scarlet evening gown out of the twenties. The first lounge was bare, shadowy; a large fireplace with a few undersized logs gave off little licks of flame without warmth, while the sultry North African wind came down the chimney with the sound of rattling dry palm fronds. This area was quite devoid of furniture except for a golden claw-footed throne and a tall wooden clothes tree as ungainly as a scarecrow. Next came a room in a symphony of blues, ranging from royal to delphinium to pale cerulean. It was dominated by a mural representing Old King Cole; beneath his crown appeared the feathered face of an owl. The last salon, octagonal in shape, was nothing but an expanse of purple and pink harem cushions. The cruisers were bewildered by the march through the weirdly changed interior of the* QE 2, *and they were relieved to reach the summit of the ship where, crowded together, they waited eagerly for the show of might to begin.*

An aircraft carrier berthed opposite the QE 2 *had a flight deck that spread as far and wide as a mall. At one end a band*

*shell resounded with martial music played with such vigor that
the young millionaires swelled with national pride. And they
realized that foreign territory was theirs to reshape, the inhabitants to be reeducated in the stronger, richer, more multitudi-
nous, technologically advanced democratic American way of
life. The antiaircraft guns, as plentiful as park benches, were
pointed in all directions. The band struck up another march and
the officers appeared from below in immaculate white summer
dress uniforms festooned in gold braid and hung with medals and
rainbow decorations. The parade circled the flight deck, everyone saluting upward toward the young millionaires. Strict order
of rank was observed, from the lowly ensign to the admiral,
with money, represented by the travelers aboard the QE 2, at
the very pinnacle. It was a stirring moment and the young
millionaires stood like royalty atop the liner to pass in review the
ceremony below.*

*Only George Gruntle was seated, although his leg brace had
been returned to him as mysteriously as it had vanished. He
had found it, along with the platinum watch, flung carelessly
outside his cabin door when they docked at Casablanca. Now,
placed well forward on a canvas captain's chair, he resembled a
Hollywood director, and the scene before him, the carrier, crew,
band, guns, looked like an old-fashioned movie location.
Nearby one might discover, in equally surreal detail, a Wild
West outpost, a Southern plantation or the biblical city of Baby-
lon.*

*The demonstration was about to start. The officers lined up
in stiff motionless rows as though posing for a yearbook gradua-
tion photograph. Guns were trained skyward and behind them
the sailors were at their posts.*

*The first cannon went off with a modest splutter and crackle
that sounded like Fourth of July fireworks. The young millionaires and their wives were reminded of home and summer: their*

houses, lawns, gardens and the sparklers released by their sons and daughters at dusk. So they responded from habit with the expected "oohs" and "ahs" that gained crescendo as the show increased in noise and brilliance.

The tropical night grew somber to receive the fountains, cascades, pinwheels and spirals of light. But between each display the sky resumed its immobile glare. It was as though the vast eye were winking in slow motion, ominously imitating the minuscule twinkle of the Christmas trees inside the hotel lobbies and the yachts. The din grew deafening, the flares blinding, and each time a gun was detonated the voyagers were revealed in livid greenish illumination. Fear was creeping up on national pride. The young millionaires and their wives wished that they had been safely back home celebrating a real Fourth of July, accustomed and manageable. The children would be sent off to bed while the adults lingered on the terraces and patios, the men discussing the stock market and taxes, the women clothes and their latest purchases. In the return of silence they could even hear the subdued reassurance of insect hum. Instead they were far away and this show was getting out of hand. Ben Newman left his place in search of the captain of the QE 2. When he found him Ben would tell him to order the admiral to stop, they had had enough. But the captain was not to be located, and Ben ran through the deserted, subterranean corridors pursued by the shattering blast of cannon discharge.

From the top of the ship the others welcomed what had to be the finale: a dazzling American flag unfurled in the heavens, accompanied by a great clap of thunder. A moment later the QE 2 was a mountain of fire rising even higher than the flag, extinguishing its Technicolor radiance. The flames assumed myriad flickering shapes: burning gargoyles, imps and four beasts, red, orange, blue and deathly pale. When at last the conflagration subsided, where the QE 2 had been there was nothing. The white walls of Casablanca, the yachts, the Sixth Fleet were all consumed and the night sky had regained its undisturbed, impassive stare.

Over the stretch of vacant sand the few remains of a civilization were strewn like garbage: a platinum watch, broken cameras, an iron brace, severed sections of machinery, twisted slot machines and a radio that was still playing. Out of it issued the evil croakings of a foghorn followed by a bland male voice, "My name is —— I am here to ask you whether you have ever thought of sailing on a cruise —— " The tone was cheerful, modulated, phrases terminating in a studied upbeat, the accent sophisticated, refined, New England preparatory school, New York City smart set. " —— you will find yourself amidst every luxury on board the S.S. —— leaving from —— arriving at —— why not put the trials and tribulations of winter behind you —— bask in sunshine near tropical seas — everything for your comfort and entertainment —— visit exotic ports with us —— upon your return your friends will be astonished by your newfound cosmopolitan culture and savoir faire —— let me urge you —— you will be delighted —— book passage now before it's too late —— join me — join us on this sensational voyage —— " The voice spoke.

Who was listening?